200
Prayers
to
ENCOURAGE
YOUR HEART

200 Prayers to ENCOURAGE YOUR HEART

INSPIRATION FOR WOMEN

LINDA HANG

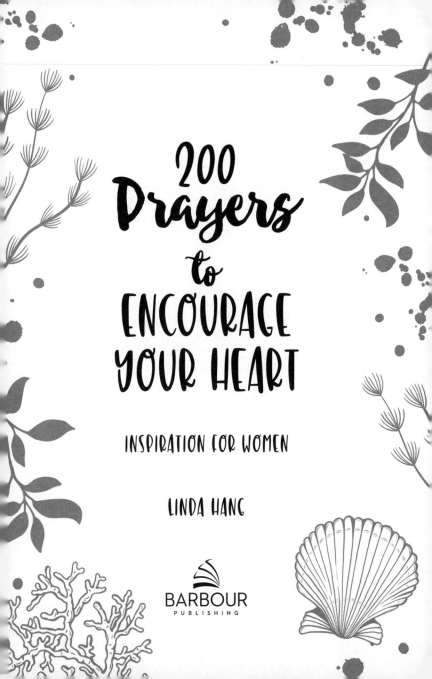

BARBOUR
PUBLISHING

Print ISBN 978-1-63609-672-8

Published by Barbour Publishing, Inc., 1810 Barbour Drive, Uhrichsville, Ohio 44683, www.barbourbooks.com

Our mission is to inspire the world with the life-changing message of the Bible.

Member of the
Evangelical Christian
Publishers Association

Printed in China.

INTRODUCTION

"I lift my eyes to you, O God, enthroned in heaven," said the psalmist (Psalm 123:1 NLT). And so can we—no matter what is taking place in our lives.

Feeling lost? Look up to the one who points out the way. At the end of your rope? Look up to the one who is reaching down with help. Need a new perspective? Look up to the one who oversees the big picture. Worn out, stressed out, or bummed out? Look up to the one who makes all things new. Burdened? Look up to the one who offers to carry every burden. Don't know where to turn? Look up to the one who is ever in front of you. Just an ordinary day? Look up anyway!

God invites us to pray. God invites us to take our eyes off our circumstances, off ourselves, and to look up. Wherever. Whenever. Forever.

May these two hundred prayers inspire you to lift your eyes to Him.

FIRST THING

Hearken unto the voice of my cry, my King, and my God: for unto thee will I pray. My voice shalt thou hear in the morning, O LORD; in the morning will I direct my prayer unto thee, and will look up.
PSALM 5:2–3 KJV

God, how well You know that I am not a morning person. I'm groggy and grouchy, and I rarely feel like talking. But the best way I know to greet the new day is to say a good-morning prayer to You. Better than hitting SNOOZE half a dozen times, better than a cup of joe, definitely better than a jog around the block are these moments of leaning my head back to feel Your radiance warming my face like sunshine, these moments of looking up to pray. Hear my voice as I begin today with a few words to You, my King and my God. Amen.

Morning prayers are great—so are midmorning prayers and afternoon prayers and evening prayers and middle-of-the-night prayers. The only time that isn't good to come to God in prayer is *never*.

7

EYES ON HIM

*Let us put every thing out of our lives that keeps us
from doing what we should. Let us keep running
in the race that God has planned for us. Let us
keep looking to Jesus. Our faith comes from Him
and He is the One Who makes it perfect.*
HEBREWS 12:1–2 NLV

Lord, sometimes this world is too much. Too much commotion. Too much stress. Too much chasing after this then that. Help me to examine my life—*truly* examine it—and remove anything that stops me from doing Your will. Help me to follow Your plan for me. Most of all, help me to look to You every day. When life pulls my eyes here, there, and everywhere, draw them back to You. You are the source of my faith, the one who will perfect my faith. I can trust You in the middle of "too much" to be just what I need. Thank You, Jesus. Amen.

Our lives are full. Lots of things grab for our
attention. But we can find our center again by
focusing on "the author and finisher of our faith"
(Hebrews 12:2 KJV). Let's fix our eyes on Him.

BEYOND IMAGINING

He took him outside and said, "Look up at the sky and count the stars—if indeed you can count them." Then he said to him, "So shall your offspring be." Abram believed the LORD, and he credited it to him as righteousness.

GENESIS 15:5–6 NIV

Lord, twice before, You told Abraham that You would make him into a great nation, that his descendants would be too numerous to count (Genesis 12:2; 13:16). When You reminded him of Your words, You used a celestial exclamation point. Abraham's reward would be very great indeed—his descendants would fill the earth like the stars filled the sky! You had big plans for this childless nomad's life, Lord, bigger than he could imagine. You have plans for my life too. I may not know what they are, but when I gaze at Your heavens, I know they are bigger than I can imagine. Amen.

Sometimes to believe God's promises we must literally look up to be reminded of God's greatness. It takes a limitless God to create and sustain our vast universe, and that same God is working in and through our lives in mighty ways.

9

TESTED

"The fire and wood are here," Isaac said, "but where is the lamb for the burnt offering?" Abraham answered, "God himself will provide the lamb for the burnt offering, my son." And the two of them went on together.
GENESIS 22:7–8 NIV

How many hours, Lord, did Abraham spend on his knees praying for a son? How long the years must have seemed as he waited for You to make Your promise a reality! But how joyous the celebration must have been as he held baby Isaac—the beginning of Your promise fulfilled! Then one day You commanded Abraham to sacrifice that long-awaited son. Only because Abraham had learned to turn to You for the impossible could he obey. You provided before; You would provide again. Lord, may my faith be as strong. May my answer to life's tests be, "God Himself will. . ." Amen.

Abraham could have disobeyed by relying on human reason—Isaac was supposed to be the first of Abraham's countless descendants, but that branch would be cut off if Isaac was dead. Instead, Abraham obeyed by trusting in God's omnipotence. God has the power to raise the dead!

BIRDS OF THE AIR

"Look at the birds in the sky. They do not plant seeds. They do not gather grain. They do not put grain into a building to keep. Yet your Father in heaven feeds them! Are you not more important than the birds?"
MATTHEW 6:26 NLV

Jesus, You told Your followers not to worry, and then You told them to look at the birds in the sky. Not one bird is worried about where dinner is coming from. They are free to soar and sing because the Father feeds them. He takes care of them. Lord, You tell me, "Do not worry," but so often I do worry. Forgive me for not trusting You. Remind me with each bird I see today that I am so very important to You. I am free to soar and sing because You take care of me. Amen.

Trusting God to provide is a choice—a choice that is a lot harder to make when our resources dwindle. But we can rely on God to meet our *every* need. When your trust level is as low as a rain gauge in August, ask God to fill you up.

IN HIS HANDS

*When people spoke against Him, He never spoke
back. When He suffered from what people did to
Him, He did not try to pay them back. He left it in the
hands of the One Who is always right in judging.*
1 PETER 2:23 NLV

Jesus, Your life is our example. We are supposed to live the way
You lived. We should also expect to face hardships because You
faced them too. Being fully God didn't mean You had it easy.
You were insulted and You suffered, yet You didn't respond
in kind. You gave those situations to Your Father. You knew
God would judge rightly, so You entrusted Your life to Him.
Help me to do the same, Jesus. When I'm treated unfairly, or
even persecuted for being a Christian, I will leave it in my
Father's hands. Amen.

Far from promising carefree lives, the Bible
guarantees that Christians will have tribulation.
That tribulation often comes from other people.
But no matter the hardship, be encouraged. Your
heavenly Father sees—and He can handle any trouble.

12

FOCAL POINT

*But Stephen, full of the Holy Spirit, looked up to heaven
and saw the glory of God, and Jesus standing at the
right hand of God. . . . While they were stoning him,
Stephen prayed, "Lord Jesus, receive my spirit."*
ACTS 7:55, 59 NIV

Lord, all Stephen did was tell the truth. When he was dragged
before the Sanhedrin, he told Your story. But because they
were full of hate, they brutally killed Stephen for his act of
faithfulness. What's amazing to me is that Stephen didn't
collapse spiritually. How? Your Word says he was full of the
Holy Spirit and looked up to see You. In life his focus was You;
in death his focus was still You. Lord, my trials are ripples
in a puddle compared to Stephen's waves, but my strength
and hope are the same. You uphold and keep me—body and
spirit! Amen.

Christians throughout history have endured
intense trials by focusing on God. Our struggles
may never be as intense, but whether it's the daily
grind or a once-in-a-lifetime event, we can follow
in their footsteps by making God our focus.

TROUBLE SHELTER

My soul goes to You to be safe. And I will be safe in the shadow of Your wings until the trouble has passed. I will cry to God Most High, to God Who finishes all things for me.
PSALM 57:1–2 NLV

Everywhere I turn, Lord, there's distress. Everywhere I look, there's bad news—global, national, local, personal. But when troubles surround me and there's nowhere to go for relief, Lord, remind me of the psalmist's words. Help me say them about my life, because they are true! My soul goes to You to be safe and finds refuge there. I will be safe in the shadow of Your wings because You encircle me with Your care until the troubles surrounding me surround me no more. I cry to You, God Most High, the one who can do all things for me! Amen.

With so much brokenness in our world,
it's easy to feel overwhelmed. But never forget:
God hasn't abandoned us, and He is an ever-present
shelter in the middle of so much brokenness.

OF GREAT WORTH

Your beauty should come from the inside.
It should come from the heart. This is the kind that
lasts. Your beauty should be a gentle and quiet
spirit. In God's sight this is of great worth.
1 PETER 3:4 NLV

God, I know what Your Word says about beauty. A woman's beauty isn't found on the outside—it's found in her heart. That's very different from what the world says. Even if we hear about "inner beauty," the images we see and the products we're sold tell us that beauty is still skin deep. I struggle with this, Lord. I want to look beautiful. But more than that, I want to be beautiful in Your sight. Your opinion, not man's, matters most. So teach my heart to value what You value. Make me beautiful in my spirit. Amen.

Peter wrote that a gentle and quiet spirit is of great worth in God's sight. In the same letter, Peter wrote that Jesus was rejected by men but of great worth in God's sight (1 Peter 2:4). It's true—man looks at the outside; God looks at the heart (1 Samuel 16:7).

TOO HARD?

Sarah laughed to herself. . . . Then the Lord said to Abraham, "Why did Sarah laugh and say, 'How can I give birth to a child when I am so old?' Is anything too hard for the Lord?"
GENESIS 18:12–14 NLV

Lord, when I read about Sarah, I wonder why she doubted. After all, You told Abraham face-to-face that he and Sarah would have a child. But Sarah was human. She was thinking with her feet on the earth and not with her head in the heavens. She thought, "I'm too old to have children," not, "God can work miracles." Yes, Sarah was human like me. How often do I forget that You are a God who works miracles? How often do I think that something is too hard for You? *Nothing* is too hard for You! Help me to believe. Amen.

When we consider the situations in our lives, let's stop putting limits on almighty God. We may not see *how* a certain outcome is possible, but we know *who* is able. With God, what is humanly impossible is divinely easy.

16

BURDEN BEARER

Humble yourselves, therefore, under God's mighty hand, that he may lift you up in due time. Cast all your anxiety on him because he cares for you.
1 PETER 5:6–7 NIV

Lord, anxiety is a burden I can't bear alone. Worse, the more I try to bear it, the more the anxiety grows. But You, Lord, don't ask me to bear my anxiety alone. You don't want me to bear it at all! I can bring my cares to You because You care about me. Help me remember that I'm not burdening You with my worries. You are mighty. You reign over this whole messy world. You're able to shoulder my anxiety. And as I give my anxiety and myself to You, You will lift me up. Thank You for taking this burden from me! Amen.

When anxiety rolls through your life like a boulder barreling its way down a hill, pray. Take hold of God's Word and His promise: "Cast your cares on the LORD and he will sustain you; he will never let the righteous be shaken" (Psalm 55:22 NIV).

HEAVEN-MINDED

If then you have been raised with Christ, keep looking for the good things of heaven. This is where Christ is seated on the right side of God. Keep your minds thinking about things in heaven. Do not think about things on the earth.
Colossians 3:1–2 nlv

Lord, You know everything I think about; all that jostles in my mind. One minute it might be family and the next minute work. Then my to-do list. Then my bills, and how much money I lack. Then that temptation I'm struggling against. And what about the future? What if I lose my job? What if something happens to a loved one? What if there's an earthquake or a war? . . . On and on and on. Lord, I forget that this life isn't the end. I have heaven to look forward to. Help me keep my mind on eternity with You. Amen.

"The way of this world will soon be gone," Paul wrote. His advice? "Live as if the world has no hold on you" (1 Corinthians 7:31 nlv). Our future is heaven. Shouldn't our thoughts match that destination?

WITH EACH STEP

In their hearts humans plan their course,
but the LORD establishes their steps.
PROVERBS 16:9 NIV

Lord, I have goals and dreams for my life. There is so much I want to do. So many places I want to go. So many things I haven't experienced yet. In my heart I plan for those things. I envision the paths I could take to lead me to my goals and dreams. But I am not the commander of my life. You are! You know every one of my plans, Lord. And You know my desires—from my loftiest hopes to my deepest longings. So I come to You with my plans. I humbly place them before You and wait for You to mark out the way ahead. Amen.

Our independent streak might fight God's sovereignty; He is sovereign nonetheless. His plans aren't always what we would choose, but they are far better than our own. The one who is above time—who sees the beginning and the end—watches over us. Trust Him with your life.

LIKE HANNAH

Hannah was very troubled. She prayed to the Lord and cried with sorrow. Then she. . .said, "O Lord of All, be sure to look on the trouble of Your woman servant, and remember me. Do not forget Your woman servant, but give me a son."
1 SAMUEL 1:10–11 NLV

God, Your people respond so differently to trials. Like Hannah, Sarah wanted a child. Unlike Hannah, she tried to get what she wanted on her own. She had Hagar sleep with Abraham, thinking that would solve the problem, but it only led to more problems. Hannah brought her troubles to *You*. She asked *You* to solve the problem—and You did! God, I am very troubled. There's a hole in my life, and I need You to fill it. So like Hannah, I pour out my heart to You. I ask You to provide, and in Your way and in Your timing, You will! Amen.

We're a DIY generation. Have a problem? Do something yourself to fix it. But our best efforts always begin with bringing our troubles to God and waiting for Him to lead.

WHAT DOES IT MEAN?

[Joseph] asked Pharaoh's officials. . ."Why do you
look so sad today?" "We both had dreams," they
answered, "but there is no one to interpret them."
Then Joseph said to them, "Do not interpretations
belong to God? Tell me your dreams."
GENESIS 40:7–8 NIV

God, throughout the Bible, You spoke to people using dreams. You revealed Your plans and what people should do. Yet those dreams didn't always make sense. Joseph turned to You to interpret dreams. You gave him the wisdom to understand them. My dreams don't always make sense, God, and they may not always be from You. But I can turn to You with all my dreams. Comfort me when I'm unsettled by the bad ones. Show me if there's any truth in the baffling ones. Encourage me with the beautiful ones. Let me tell You my dreams. Amen.

Lots of people claim to know the meaning of dreams, but only God truly knows. Take your dreams to God in prayer and leave the interpretations where they belong—with Him.

WITH HIS HELP

"With the faithful You show Yourself faithful....
For by You I can run through an army.
By my God I can jump over a wall."
2 SAMUEL 22:26, 30 NLV

David was no stranger to difficulties, Lord. So he had learned to count on one true source of help—the God who had proved He was faithful through all those difficulties. With You by his side, David could do incredible things. Lord, I likely won't face down an entire army or have to leap walls. But whatever confronts me, I can overcome it. As long as You stand beside me, I can do incredible things. In every difficulty, I will call out to You, faithful one. Please help me to be as faithful to You as You are to me. Amen.

What difficulties must you run through or jump over right now? You could go it alone or you could go to God. Remember: our faithful Lord is forever ready to hear our prayers for help.

FOOLED!

The people of Gibeon heard what Joshua had done to Jericho and Ai. So they went out to fool him, as men from another land. . . . The men of Israel took some of their food. They did not ask the Lord what they should do.
JOSHUA 9:3–4, 14 NLV

Lord, Your command was straightforward. The Israelites were supposed to kill all the inhabitants of the land You gave them to be their own. That included the Gibeonites. But the Gibeonites tried to trick Joshua into making peace with them, and it worked because the Israelites acted without asking for Your advice. Lord, real-life decisions aren't always clear when I lose sight of You. I know what Your Word says. Then the enemy tries to trick me, and I act without asking. I end up going against Your Word. Forgive me for my disobedience. May I pray to You *first*. Amen.

Our enemy, Satan, is a wily one. Like the Gibeonites, he is skilled at deception. A certain choice might *seem* okay, but we can be *sure* if we seek God's counsel. He will help us through every dilemma.

THROUGH SUFFERING

So if God wants you to suffer, give yourself to Him. He will do what is right for you. He made you and He is faithful.
1 PETER 4:19 NLV

God, I don't like to suffer. Who does? Suffering is uncomfortable, taxing, wearisome—a whole list of adjectives, and not one of them good. But Your Word doesn't view suffering as altogether bad. You turn ugly into beautiful in Your time. Through suffering we become more like Christ. Help me come to You in my suffering. Help me share how I'm really feeling, and then remind me of Your Word. I can give myself to You with confidence. You, my loving Father, have my best interests in mind. You, my faithful Creator, will never let me down. Amen.

In the middle of suffering, we can't always see the ways God is shaping us as His children, but we can see it after the fact. To get through current suffering, think back on past suffering. What good came from the bad then? God is just as faithful now.

FAITH FROM ABOVE

I am writing to those who have received the same faith as ours which is of great worth and which no amount of money can buy. This faith comes from our God and Jesus Christ, the One Who saves.
2 PETER 1:1 NLV

Lord, my faith is so important to me. Without my faith I would be lost in sin. Without my faith I would walk this earth alone. Without my faith I wouldn't have answers to "Why?" Without my faith I wouldn't have hope for tomorrow. But You, wonderful Lord, looked down from heaven and chose to give me that faith. Thank You! Life may test my faith, Lord, but I know that the source of my faith will secure my faith as I look up to You in prayer. Again I say thank You! Please fill me with faith today. Amen.

"Just have faith!" Faith can carry us through life's challenges, but drumming up enough of it on our own is a challenge in itself. Our faith came from God—let's look to Him to keep us faith-full.

LIGHT IN THE DARK

What the early preachers said was true. . . . Listen until you understand what they have said. Then it will be like the morning light which takes away the darkness. And the Morning Star (Christ) will rise to shine in your hearts.
2 PETER 1:19 NLV

Jesus, we need Your light shining in our lives because this is a dark world. We would never find our way to the Father in the darkness—we'd just grope around for a while and wind up where we started. But You have revealed Your truth to us through the scriptures. You have lit the path to Yourself, our Savior! I don't understand everything in Your Word, so I'll bring my questions to You and ask the Holy Spirit to help me see. Then one glorious day—when You return—there will be no more questions. Your light will expel *all* darkness. Amen.

Studying the Old Testament is sometimes a daunting task. But God has not left us without help. He sent the helper— the Holy Spirit—to teach us all things (John 14:26). When you're looking for answers, He's the best place to start.

SHINING FOR GOD

*"In the same way, let your light shine before
others, that they may see your good deeds
and glorify your Father in heaven."*
MATTHEW 5:16 NIV

Lord, I get such joy from serving others and sharing the good news. Sometimes doing those things is difficult, but it also makes me feel good about myself. I'll admit, it can even make me prideful. If I'm not careful, selfless acts become opportunities for people to look at me and what I've done. Lord, You tell me to let my light shine. Yet as I obey Your words, I need to remember that letting my light shine is never about me. It's about glorifying You. May others see my good deeds and look at You, Lord. All glory to You! Amen.

Getting into the habit of praying about our ministries can center our efforts on God. Talk over your good deeds with Him. Give your work and the glory to Him. After all, our light shines brightest when His power flows through us.

HE RESCUES!

So you see, the Lord knows how to rescue godly people from their trials, even while keeping the wicked under punishment until the day of final judgment.
2 PETER 2:9 NLT

Lord, at times life feels like an ocean. I'm swimming strong and steady, or maybe floating for a while to enjoy the sun on my skin, but then the waves of trials come. They could be hardships or temptations, but suddenly I'm fighting to stay above the water. I barely catch my breath before another wave crashes down. In those moments, Lord, I raise my hand toward the sky, and You reach out and rescue me. I cry to You in prayer, and You answer my call for help. Thank You for being so near. Thank You for knowing just how to save me. Amen.

God preserves His people during earthly trials
that the enemy intends to use for our destruction.
God will also deliver the godly from ultimate
judgment. He is our rescuer—now to eternity!

A WHOLE NEW WORLD

We are looking for what God has promised,
which are new heavens and a new earth.
Only what is right and good will be there.
2 PETER 3:13 NLV

Lord, what a mess we've made of this world! You created the earth and said that it was good. You made a paradise for humans, but sin marred paradise. Ever since that day when Eve and Adam ate the fruit, sin has been eating away at Your creation. Lord, this messy world is too much for me today. All I see is what is wrong. I need to hear Your promise that there is hope, that You will make things right. One day You will create a new heaven and a new earth. And once again You will say that it is good. Amen.

The new heaven and the new earth that we read about in the Bible are *real*. We will live in God's new creation as believers in Christ. Take a break from this world and imagine the one to come.

READY AND WAITING

"See! I am coming soon. . . . See! I am coming soon. . . . Yes, I am coming soon!"
REVELATION 22:7, 12, 20 NLV

Lord, three times at the end of Your revelation to John, You announced that You were coming soon. What was true in John's day is true now. Lord, You have promised to come again to establish Your kingdom. You have promised to come again to reward Your followers. One day You will fulfill that promise, just as You fulfill every one of Your promises. Help me keep my eyes open for You. Help me to be watching for Your return. And while I wait, help me be obedient, because to the one who obeys, You promise happiness (Revelation 22:7). Come, Lord Jesus! Amen.

The Bible says that Christ's return will come
like a thief in the night—unexpectedly. But as
Christians, we won't be surprised by that day.
Our Lord has told us He's coming. Let's be ready!

FOREVERMORE

We do not look at the things that can be seen.
We look at the things that cannot be seen.
The things that can be seen will come to an end.
But the things that cannot be seen will last forever.
2 CORINTHIANS 4:18 NLV

Lord, sometimes—okay, maybe a lot of times—I cling to stuff instead of spirit. I depend on earthly things for my happiness, security, self-esteem. . . But buying everything I want won't buy happiness. A bigger savings account won't save me from worries. Being selfie perfect won't guarantee a picture-perfect life. The truth is I'll never find lasting happiness, security, or anything else from earthly things. They will end. Lord, I need Your help with this. Help me live for treasures in heaven. Help me seek and hold on to You above all things. Because that will go on forever. Amen.

Making our way through this life is much easier
if we are able to look beyond it. How do we see
these invisible things? We ask God to show us.

FIRST OFF

*"Your Father in heaven knows you need all these things.
First of all, look for the holy nation of God. Be right with
Him. All these other things will be given to you also."*
MATTHEW 6:32–33 NLV

God, thank You for knowing us so well! When Jesus told us
how to live, He paired the command with assurance. He said
not to worry about clothes or food; He said to put You first.
But He knew we'd struggle. So He reminded us that You see
what we need and will supply it. God, my relationship with
You is the number one, top priority in my life. And as I put
You first, I have Your promise that You will take care of the
rest. Help me be right with You, God, first and foremost. I
leave my needs in Your hands. Amen.

Because physical needs are so immediate, we think
to put them first. But God tells us to prioritize *Him.*
Why? Because when our soul is secure, so is our life.

YET WILL I

"Though he slay me, yet will I hope in him; I will surely defend my ways to his face. Indeed, this will turn out for my deliverance, for no godless person would dare come before him!"
JOB 13:15–16 NIV

Lord, Job suffered tremendously. He lost just about everything: his livelihood, his children, his health. His wife even encouraged him to curse You and die! But Job hadn't lost his faith. He trusted You even if times of blessing suddenly turned to times of trouble—even if You killed him. Job knew he was a believer and innocent, and that gave him confidence to take this case to You. Lord, that same confidence is mine as well. Thank You that I can come before You as Your redeemed daughter. Through the worst times, I will hope in You! Amen.

Job was a godly man, so we might see his situation as unjust. Job himself continued to believe in a just God. Job was willing to accept both good and bad from God (Job 2:10) because he had faith that God could do nothing but what was right.

THIRST QUENCHER

*As the deer desires rivers of water, so my soul desires
You, O God. My soul is thirsty for God, for the living
God. When will I come and meet with God?*
PSALM 42:1–2 NLV

Lord, the psalmist's soul longed for You, and he sought You to quench that thirst. You promise rivers of living water to anyone who comes to You. Lord, my soul is thirsty. I don't always recognize my own thirst though. I feel "off" and try to explain it away, or I fill my life with so many things that distract me. But what I really need is a deep drink of You. Thank You for pouring Yourself into me each time I kneel before You. My soul is thirsty *for You*, God. When will I come and meet with You again? Amen.

If our only communion with God is a quick prayer every now and then, our souls are dehydrated! Just as our bodies need water to thrive—and survive—our souls need God. Make meeting with Him a regular part of your day.

DON'T LOOK AWAY

*Then Peter got down out of the boat, walked on the water
and came toward Jesus. But when he saw the wind, he was
afraid and, beginning to sink, cried out, "Lord, save me!"*
MATTHEW 14:29–30 NIV

Lord, the sight of You walking on the wind-tossed sea must
have been amazing enough. Then Peter opened his mouth.
His way of checking that it was actually You walking on the
water was to walk on the water himself at Your command.
You commanded; he walked. All went swimmingly until he
looked away from You. The sight of the wind caused him to
sink. Lord, when I look around at the troubles in life, I'm
afraid. I see the "winds," and I sink. Steady my eyes on You so
that I do not sink. Thank You for saving me when I do. Amen.

Our faith is often shaky when we focus on everything
else *but* God. Our faith is secure when we turn our
eyes toward Him. He is the one who enables us to
get through waves and smooth waters alike.

A HEAVENLY LESSON

"Yes, he humbled you by letting you go hungry and then feeding you with manna. . . . He did it to teach you that people do not live by bread alone; rather, we live by every word that comes from the mouth of the LORD."

DEUTERONOMY 8:3 NLT

Lord, even after the Israelites turned away from You, You didn't turn away from them. You continued to shepherd them. They would not enter the Promised Land because of their disobedience, but still You wanted Your children to *learn* from their wandering. You wanted to teach them about Yourself and about living. You wanted them to grow closer to You. Lord, You use hardships to form me too. You use even the years that seem wasted to help me know You better. And I've learned, Lord. I've learned that I don't live by bread alone—but through the bread of life. Amen.

The Israelites' physical sustenance came from heaven those forty years in the wilderness. But God was doing more than teaching them to look up for their food. He was teaching them to look up at the source of life itself.

YOUR CHOICE

Use the silver to buy whatever you like: cattle, sheep, wine or other fermented drink, or anything you wish. Then you and your household shall eat there in the presence of the LORD your God and rejoice.
DEUTERONOMY 14:26 NIV

Lord, every time I read this verse in Deuteronomy, I'm reminded of how loving You are, how You created each of us as individuals, and how You care about each of us individually—even when we're worshipping *You*. You instructed the Israelites to eat a portion of their produce in Your presence. If the place You chose was too far to take their offering with them, they could buy whatever they liked. You left what they bought up to them because they were celebrating *with* You. Lord, I thank You and praise You for Your tender care. Amen.

God is concerned with our good because He is full of goodness. We find reminders of our Father's care and character throughout the Bible. We don't deserve such attention, but God loves us just the same.

THE LORD'S JOY

And Nehemiah continued, "Go and celebrate. . . .
This is a sacred day before our Lord. Don't be dejected
and sad, for the joy of the LORD is your strength!"
NEHEMIAH 8:10 NLT

Lord, the people had just heard all the ways they had sinned
against You. What's more, the days ahead wouldn't suddenly
be easy after rebuilding the wall around Jerusalem. Their
faces probably drooped. But Nehemiah encouraged them to
be happy. It was a day of rejoicing, and above all, the joy of the
Lord was their strength. That was no pat statement—it was
truth. Lord, there is always a reason to hope in You. I may sin,
but You forgive. I may face trouble, but You work all things
for good. In any situation, Your joy is my strength. Amen!

The joy of the Lord is our strength. Believe it.
Some situations in life bring us down, yes.
But the joy that comes from the Lord holds us up.

FOLLOW HIS LEAD

In all the travels of the Israelites, whenever the cloud lifted from above the tabernacle, they would set out; but if the cloud did not lift, they did not set out—until the day it lifted.
EXODUS 40:36–37 NIV

Lord, You led the Israelites faithfully for forty years, and they waited for You to lead. The Bible says they set out when the cloud lifted and stayed put when it did not lift. Were there days, weeks, months when they stayed in one place, wondering when they would move on? But as soon as that cloud lifted, they knew it was time to pull up stakes. Sometimes I wish Your leading in my life was so simple. Lead me, Lord, in Your own way. Help me be aware of Your guiding hand. Show me when and where to go. Amen.

The more time we spend praying and listening
to God, the clearer we will hear His guidance.
The closer we stay to His side, the more keenly
we will sense the shepherd leading in our lives.

TRUSTING IN THE LORD

*Trust in the LORD with all your heart, and do
not lean on your own understanding.*
PROVERBS 3:5 ESV

Lord, often my understanding leaves me wobbly—like a three-legged chair. For a time, and if I sit on it just right, it may stay upright. But eventually it will tip. One unexpected event. One unexplained situation—that's all it takes to unsettle me. I can't lean on my own understanding; I can lean on You. You, Lord, are dependable. You control the mightiest wave with a word and command the tiniest fly with a whistle. You see the end of all things from the beginning. Nothing is beyond You. When I begin to trust my understanding, remind me of who You are so that I trust in You with my whole heart. Amen.

When we depend on our own understanding,
life is confusing. Thankfully, God is our clarity.
We won't fully understand, not everything;
but we can fully trust in the Lord.

POWER UP

*He answered me, "I am all you need. I give
you My loving-favor. My power works best in
weak people." I am happy to be weak and have
troubles so I can have Christ's power in me.*
2 CORINTHIANS 12:9 NLV

Lord, Paul wrote about feeling weak and asking You to take away the source of his weakness. Wanting to feel strong isn't just a macho thing; we women want to feel powerful too. Yes, I can juggle the career, the family, the social life, and the dozen grocery bags—and look good doing it! Then the doctor's diagnosis comes. Or the demanding boss. Or any number of troubles that make me feel powerless. But that weakness is actually something to rejoice in. When I reach the end of my strength, Yours has only begun! Lord, strengthen me with *Your* power today. Amen.

Feeling strong can breed self-reliance—to the point where we don't think we need God. But feeling weak teaches us God-reliance. Then, even in our weakness, we are strong (2 Corinthians 12:10). Christ's power empowers us!

THE ONLY ONE

As for God, His way is perfect. The Word of the Lord has stood the test. He is a covering for all who go to Him for a safe place. For Who is God, but the Lord? And who is a rock except our God?

God, nothing compares to You. Nothing is higher than You. Nothing is holier than You. Nothing is better than You. You alone are God. And what a God You are! The psalmist's words sing out about You: Your way is perfect. Your Word is proven. You protect us when we enter Your presence. God, I don't always praise You the way I should. I don't always give You the place You deserve. That sounds absurd, saying it now. For who else is God but You? Who else is a rock except You? Forgive me, my Lord. Thank You for being a God like no other. Amen.

If God has been a part of our lives for a while, we may forget that God grants us an amazing privilege—fellowship with Him, the one true God. Let's not take a single prayer for granted!

BE HOLY

*Be holy in every part of your life. Be like the
Holy One Who chose you. The Holy Writings
say, "You must be holy, for I am holy."*
1 PETER 1:15–16 NLV

God, I don't have to look far to find examples to pattern my life after. Just about everywhere—from the people in my life to posts on the internet—I see opinions on how to live. But Your Word is clear: the pattern for our lives is You. I am supposed to be like You, God, and You are holy. Being holy doesn't come naturally to me—far from it. But just as I look to You for the pattern, I'll look to You for the power to become holy. Make me holy in every part of my life, I pray. Amen.

The reason for being holy isn't only about us.
Our lives reflect our God. We worship and honor
God by living holy lives as a witness to Him.

ONCE BEGUN. . .

I am sure that God Who began the good
work in you will keep on working in you
until the day Jesus Christ comes again.
PHILIPPIANS 1:6 NLV

God, You know how I struggle to keep going when the work is tedious or difficult. I get tired or bored. Or I get discouraged. It would be easy to stop and move on to something else. I'm so thankful that *You* don't stop the work You've started. You don't give up on us, even when we're stubborn or whiny or forgetful. You began a good work, and You'll continue that good work. You began changing us into Christ's likeness, and You'll continue until the image is complete. Open my eyes and prep my heart for the work You're doing today. Amen.

God is perfecting us. His goal is holiness in the long run, not always happiness in the moment. When God's good work in you feels less than good to you, recall God's promises and His faithfulness.

THINK ABOUT YOUR THOUGHTS

Finally, brothers and sisters, whatever is true, whatever is noble, whatever is right, whatever is pure, whatever is lovely, whatever is admirable—if anything is excellent or praiseworthy—think about such things.
PHILIPPIANS 4:8 NIV

God, You know every one of my thoughts. That makes me cringe sometimes. You know my good thoughts, but also the not-so-good ones. You even know the downright sinful ones. What I choose to think about isn't always true, noble, right, pure, lovely, and admirable. I *want* to think about those things. But I can't do it on my own. God, as I come to You in prayer, renew my mind so that my thoughts become higher thoughts. When my mind strays to thoughts that would not please You, nudge—no, *jab* my spirit. Bring *Your* thoughts to my mind. Amen.

What we think about matters. Our minds can't dwell on ungodly thoughts without the residue showing up in our lives. So heed God's Word: "Guard your heart, for everything you do flows from it" (Proverbs 4:23 NIV).

45

ANXIOUS NO MORE

The Lord is near. Do not be anxious about anything,
but in every situation, by prayer and petition,
with thanksgiving, present your requests to God.
PHILIPPIANS 4:5–6 NIV

Lord, I'm a worrier. One tiny thought starts circling my mind and gets bigger and bigger—like a wad of cotton candy being spun round and round, only not as sweet. Soon that one tiny worry becomes a mass of anxiety. But everything I'm worrying about I should be praying about. Your Word tells me to quash any anxious thought by talking to You in every situation. You are so near to me, Lord, a breath away. Without moving at all, I'm in Your presence, where I can let You know what's on my mind. Thank You for hearing my pleas, Lord. Amen.

Anxious thought patterns can be learned—
and so can prayer patterns. It takes practice and
patience, but as prayer becomes our default
setting, peace replaces worry in our hearts.

PEACE INCOMPREHENSIBLE

The peace of God is much greater than the human mind can understand. This peace will keep your hearts and minds through Christ Jesus.
<small>PHILIPPIANS 4:7 NLV</small>

Lord, peace seems impossible right now. With all that is going on and going wrong in my world—well, I just can't calm my mind or my body. I'm uneasy. So I come to You today asking for *Your* peace. You make streams flow in the desert, Lord. You give peace where there shouldn't be any peace. Fill me with the peace that is much greater than I can understand. Let it wash over me like lapping water lulling me to serenity. *Despite* all that is going on and going wrong, Your peace will keep me, and I will be at ease. Amen.

Peace is ours in any situation. Any. But it must come from God. We can't explain His peace—it's well beyond our comprehension!—but we can surely feel its touch.

WISDOM FOR THE ASKING

If any of you lacks wisdom, you should ask God, who gives generously to all without finding fault, and it will be given to you. But when you ask, you must believe and not doubt.
JAMES 1:5–6 NIV

Lord, I don't know what I should do in this situation. I don't know what my next steps are. My first thought is to talk over the situation with a friend. That's what I usually do. But Your Word tells me to do something different when I need wisdom. When I don't know what to do, the first thing I should do is seek Your face. I should come to You and ask for the wisdom I lack. You promise to give *generously*. You promise not to find fault. So here I am asking—and believing—that You will answer. Amen.

James wrote that we must not doubt that God will give us His wisdom. . . . Before we ask for wisdom, we might need to pray for the faith to believe.

HUMBLY I PRAY

So give yourselves to God. . . . Come close to God and He will come close to you. . . . Let yourself be brought low before the Lord. Then He will lift you up and help you.
JAMES 4:7–8, 10 NLV

Lord, You will lift me up and help me no matter where I find myself. So, when I'm mired in temptation or even bobbing in the wake of sin, it's to You I should go. But there's a way I should go too. Humbly. "Give yourselves"—that's what the Bible says. "Let yourself be brought low." You won't rectify until I recognize where I'm wrong, Lord. Today I'm not coming to You with my head held high but bowed in surrender. As I come close to You, come close to me. As I drop to my knees, lift me up and help me. Amen.

Owning up to our faults is bitter. But to truly seek God's help, we must truly see ourselves. We are sinners, and He is holy. We are sinners, but Jesus is our Savior. In the end, humility is oh so sweet!

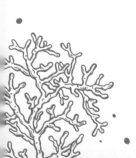

CONFESS!

*If we tell Him our sins, He is faithful and we
can depend on Him to forgive us of our sins.
He will make our lives clean from all sin.*
1 JOHN 1:9 NLV

Lord, when I know I have sinned, I don't want to face it. I want to ignore it—maybe it will just go away on its own. I want to make excuses—maybe I couldn't help it. Or I want to downplay it—maybe it wasn't *that* bad. But covering up sin isn't what *You* want. You want me to come to You. You know when I have sinned. You are also faithful to forgive when I tell You my sins. Lord, I need to confess. I need to make a clean break with sin so that You will make my life clean again. Amen.

"If we say that we have no sin, we lie to ourselves"
(1 John 1:8 NLV). Our sins exist whether we
acknowledge them or not. Denying them does no
good, but telling God our sins does a world of good.

FOR OUR GOOD

*We know that God makes all things work
together for the good of those who love Him
and are chosen to be a part of His plan.*
ROMANS 8:28 NLV

God, I read this verse in Romans and I want to believe that
the promise is true for my life, that all things work together
for my good as Your daughter. Looking at my life right now,
I'm hard pressed to see how that's possible. The things that
are bad just seem bad to me, but that's where I'm missing
it, isn't it? *To me* the things seem irreparably bad, but *You
make* all things work together for good. I don't know how
You'll do it, Lord, but I know that You will. I'll be looking to
You for good things. Amen.

Our lives don't end when this life ends, and God's
providence isn't limited to this life either.
The good He is working together may begin on
earth's soil, but it continues on heaven's shore.

THE GREAT GIVER

What shall we say about such wonderful things as these?...
Since he did not spare even his own Son but gave him
up for us all, won't he also give us everything else?
ROMANS 8:31–32 NLT

God, sometimes the truth that Christ died for sinners is so familiar that I forget how special it is. The completely innocent one died for totally undeserving ones like me. Because You loved us, You sacrificed Your Son to make us Your children too. That's wonderful enough, God, but You give us more! You don't leave us on our own for anything we need to live out Your will. I thank You for guiding and keeping me. For filling me with hope and peace. For not sparing Your Son. God, I thank You for all that You give. Amen.

A God who lavishly and graciously offered
His Son for our redemption won't be stingy
with the lesser things. No, He lavishly and
graciously gives us everything else too.

SUPER-CONQUERORS

In all these things we are more than
conquerors through him who loved us.
ROMANS 8:37 NIV

Lord, many things could defeat me in life. Temptations could make me cave. Danger could make me cower. Trials could make me lose faith. Hardships could make me lose hope. Challenges could make me quit altogether. But they *won't*. Your Word promises that in all these things that could defeat me, I am more than a conqueror because of *You*. You, the conqueror of death, now make me a conqueror of life. Your love sees me through the temptations, the danger, the trials, the hardships, the challenges; I come through victorious every time! Amen.

Romans 8:37 might sound overly optimistic,
but the apostle Paul wrote from experience when
he penned those words. From beatings to prison to
a shipwreck, he conquered his share of obstacles,
and he owed all of his victories to Christ.

WORDLESS PRAYERS

The Holy Spirit helps us where we are weak.
We do not know how to pray or what we should
pray for, but the Holy Spirit prays to God for us
with sounds that cannot be put into words.
ROMANS 8:26 NLV

Holy Spirit, words won't come today. But You know what is on my heart. You know how to express it to God. Please pray for me. Please pray what can't be put into words. Amen.

In times of strain or pain, sometimes the only thing we can do is sit silently with God. That's okay! The Spirit helps where we are weak. He prays on our behalf.

A LITTLE OIL + A LOT OF POWER

They took the jars to her, and she poured. When the jars were full, she said to her son, "Bring me another jar." And he said to her, "There is not one jar left."
2 KINGS 4:5–6 NLV

Lord, only You could have multiplied this widow's oil. She had no means to pay her husband's debt and prevent her sons from being taken away; she had just one tiny jar of oil. But You have great power. Elisha told the widow to collect empty jars and begin filling them with the oil from her jar. The oil kept flowing and flowing until she had more than enough to pay the debt owed. Lord, You provide in such creative, miraculous, and abundant ways. Today I'm feeling desperate like that widow. Please pour out Your provision as only You can. Amen.

As part of Elisha's instructions, he told the widow to fill the jars behind the closed doors of her home. Why? Because then there was no doubt who was behind the miracle—God Himself.

STREAMS IN HIS HAND

*The king's heart is a stream of water in the hand
of the LORD; he turns it wherever he will.*
PROVERBS 21:1 ESV

Lord, evil people are everywhere, and some of those evil people lead nations. Reading the headlines is enough to make me shudder sometimes. Is evil out of control? Can corrupt rulers rule unchecked? No. Your Word reassures me with the truth: You are sovereign. Just as You set boundaries for the seas at the beginning of this world, You direct the hearts of kings like streams of water until the end of this world. No ruler takes You by surprise or thwarts You. I place my trust in You—the King of all kings, the Lord of all lives. Amen.

God uses godly leaders to further His plans; He also uses evil leaders. We see it throughout the Bible. We may not be able to see it as clearly in our times, but God still rules over every ruler. God has not abdicated—and never will.

ABSOLUTELY PERFECT

*You will keep the man in perfect peace whose
mind is kept on You, because he trusts in You.*
ISAIAH 26:3 NLV

Perfect peace. Lord, Your promise isn't for a bare-bones peace that's barely enough. It's not a hit-or-miss peace that might not get us through. This peace is *perfect*. Complete. Constant. Coming only from You. *You* keep me in that perfect peace. But I have to keep my mind on You. No wonder my peace is less than perfect, Lord. So often I'm thinking of many other things besides You, the one in whom I can trust. Lord, You know what I'm keeping my mind on. I'm praying for Your help to keep it on You instead. I'm praying for Your perfect peace. Amen.

"Trust in the LORD forever, for the LORD, the LORD himself, is the Rock eternal" (Isaiah 26:4 NIV). With our minds fixed on the Rock, nothing can shake our peace!

I'LL KEEP PRAYING FOR YOU

Pray in the Spirit on all occasions with all kinds of prayers and requests. With this in mind, be alert and always keep on praying for all the Lord's people.
EPHESIANS 6:18 NIV

Lord, Your Word encourages me to come to You all the time with all kinds of prayers. You want me to pray for all Your people, not just myself. Sometimes I struggle to pray for others because I don't know exactly what they need. I don't always know how to pray for them. But whether I'm praying for myself or for others, I'm supposed to pray in the Spirit. The Holy Spirit—who knows exactly what every Christian needs and always knows how to pray for them—He helps me pray. Today in Your Spirit, I lift Your people to You. Amen.

Writing down the names of people you're praying for can remind you to keep praying. Even if you don't know specifics, God does. Pray for the Lord's people. Pray with the help of His Spirit.

DON'T STOP PRAYING

*Be happy in your hope. Do not give up when trouble
comes. Do not let anything stop you from praying.*
ROMANS 12:12 NLV

Lord, troubles are wearing me down. It's a struggle to get
through the hours. Worse, it's a struggle to pray. Sometimes I
don't even feel like praying at all. Thank You for this reminder
in Your Word. I shouldn't let *anything* stop me from praying.
Not fatigue, not discouragement, not troubles. In fact, prayer
is my lifeblood. Connection with You, Lord, is what sustains
me when trouble comes. Communion with You is what lets me
hope, lets me be happy. As I wake each day, may my prayers
be foremost in my mind. May my prayers carry me through
the days ahead. Amen.

Paul wanted to pass on practical instruction to
the early Roman church. He knew that difficult
times are made even more difficult when we
neglect our prayers. His trio of advice? "Rejoice
in. . .hope. Be patient in trouble, and *keep on
praying*" (Romans 12:12 NLT, emphasis added).

SLOTH-LESS

Do not be lazy but always work hard.
Work for the Lord with a heart full of love for Him.
ROMANS 12:11 NLV

Lord, You commanded Your people to rest one day out of seven (Exodus 16:23). Your Word says that rising at the crack of dawn and burning the midnight oil to work is in vain (Psalm 127:2). I'll admit, it's not difficult for me to obey when You tell me to rest; but when You tell me to work hard, I often want to be lazy. I'd rather put off work and play instead. In those moments of laziness, I'll ask for Your help, for Your energy to work hard. I'll remember that I'm working for You, Lord, and out of my love for You. Amen.

Laziness does more than waste time. It opens doors for evil: "Idle hands are the devil's workshop" (Proverbs 16:27 TLB). But serving God with zeal, whether during our nine-to-five or our free time, spreads God's goodness.

ESCAPE ROUTE

*God is faithful. He will not allow the temptation to
be more than you can stand. When you are tempted,
he will show you a way out so that you can endure.*
1 Corinthians 10:13 nlt

Father, temptations are hard to resist. Certain temptations
seem *impossible* to resist. But that isn't true, even if it feels
true, because You are faithful. You won't allow any temptation to be too much for me. So why do I give in to temptation
sometimes? Maybe I'm not looking where I should be looking. When I'm tempted, I tend to focus on what I'm trying to
resist, and that only makes it harder to resist. I need to turn
my attention to You instead. I need to call out to You. In every
temptation, You are with me, pointing the way out. Amen.

God makes a way out of temptation every time,
but we must be willing to go His way. Prayer *before*
we're tempted aligns our hearts with God and
trains them to seek Him *when* we're tempted.

61

OUR DEFENSE

"O Nebuchadnezzar, we do not need to defend ourselves
before you. If we are thrown into the blazing furnace,
the God whom we serve is able to save us. . . . But even
if he doesn't. . .we will never serve your gods."
DANIEL 3:16–18 NLT

God, these three men—Shadrach, Meshach, and Abednego—
were in one intense trial. Nebuchadnezzar demanded they
bow down to his gold statue. He demanded to know what
god could save them if they refused. But they didn't buckle.
They didn't beg or bargain. They didn't even need to defend
themselves—because You would defend them Yourself. You
are the same God to this day. Whatever trials I'm in, I can say
just as confidently that the God whom I serve is able to save
me. But even if You don't, I'll still worship You alone. Amen.

Although our trials may never be as fiery as Shadrach,
Meshach, and Abednego's, we still can model their faith.
They believed God would do the impossible—"He will
rescue us" (v. 17 NLT)—but entrusted the outcome to Him.

JUST WATCH!

Moses told the people, "Don't be afraid. Just stand
still and watch the LORD rescue you today.
The Egyptians you see today will never be seen again."
EXODUS 14:13 NLT

Lord, some events in my life are intimidating, but what must it have been like that day at the Red Sea? The Israelites had put Egypt behind them, and then suddenly Pharaoh was back. They were caught between an army and a watery place. When they couldn't go forward or backward, Moses told them to look up. You would deliver them. You parted the sea! Lord, when a situation seems like a horde of chariots headed toward me and I don't know what I'm going to do, I will remember that You are God. You work in mighty ways, ways I never would dream of. Amen.

The Red Sea crossing was orchestrated by God to show His deity. God sometimes puts us in difficult situations to teach us about Himself. Where is He telling you to step aside and watch Him?

THY WILL BE DONE

[Jesus] said, "Father, if it can be done,
take away what must happen to Me. Even so,
not what I want, but what You want."
LUKE 22:42 NLV

Father, Jesus must have prayed countless prayers to You, His Father. You know every single word He prayed. Here I have a glimpse of just a few, but in these few words I see how I can pray to You, my Father. Jesus didn't elaborate or embellish; He didn't even explain how He felt. He simply asked for what He wanted while surrendering to what *You* wanted. Father, You know the deep burdens and desires I'm carrying. I lay my prayers at Your feet and ask You to answer favorably. But *even so*, I rest in what You want. Amen.

Christ was in agony over His crucifixion; He prayed
so intensely that His sweat fell like drops of blood
(Luke 22:44). He asked for the cross to be taken
away, but God's answer was the cross. When God
says no, will we still say, "Your will be done"?

THE ONE THING

"Martha, Martha," the Lord answered, "you are worried and upset about many things, but few things are needed—or indeed only one. Mary has chosen what is better, and it will not be taken away from her."

LUKE 10:41–42 NIV

Lord, Martha was preoccupied with preparations; Mary was preoccupied with You. Mary recognized what was important right then: fellowship with You. The other things could wait. Every time I read this account, I wish I were like Mary, but more often I'm like Martha—especially in the mornings. I wake up, and my brain starts thinking about all the things I have to do, and then my body starts doing all the things I have to do, when what I need most is to pray. Lord, remind me to put aside my worries when You call me to spend time with You. Amen.

God knows that we have obligations in our homes,
jobs, and communities that are important.
He also knows that without our eyes on Him,
we will miss out on what is better!

DEAD TO SIN, ALIVE TO GOD

The death [Christ] died, he died to sin once for all;
but the life he lives, he lives to God. In the same way,
count yourselves dead to sin but alive to God in Christ Jesus.
ROMANS 6:10–11 NIV

Lord, thank You for breaking sin's hold on us. Before I believed in You, sin defined me. I was a sinner and nothing else, and I would have died in my sin if it were not for You. But You offered redemption, a new life. I am now a sinner turned saint, saved by Your love. Lord, my life isn't sinless, yet sin will never again be my boss. I look to You, my master. Show me how to live through and for You. Help me seek Your higher ways as I count myself dead to sin and alive to God. Amen.

We were once bound by sin and bound for hell,
but Christ broke the bonds. He severed the
chains. He freed our feet to walk with Him.

PRESS ON!

One thing I do: Forgetting what is behind and
straining toward what is ahead, I press on
toward the goal to win the prize for which God
has called me heavenward in Christ Jesus.
PHILIPPIANS 3:13–14 NIV

Lord, I need to make Paul's words my own. I need to forget what is behind and strain toward what is ahead. Right now, I keep looking back at mistakes I've made, at missed opportunities—and what I see is discouraging. It's keeping me rooted in place, unable—or maybe unwilling—to move forward. But You want me to *press on*. You want me to pursue Christlikeness day by day by day, just as You are at work in me day by day by day. Help me keep my eyes on what You are doing. Help me keep my eyes on the prize. Amen.

Paul knew he fell short of Christ's perfection,
but he pressed on because he had confidence
in the one who had claimed him as His own
(Philippians 3:12) and would one day make him
perfect—Christ Himself. The same goes for us!

HOPE

But as for me, I will always have hope and I will praise You more and more. My mouth will tell about how right and good You are and about Your saving acts all day long. For there are more than I can know.
PSALM 71:14–15 NLV

Lord, there are so many reasons to be discouraged, so many ways this world is without hope. *But as for me*—those were the psalmist's words—*I will always have hope.* As Your daughter, I will always have hope because my hope comes from You. You are right, and You are good. Your acts are marvelous! Lord, when all I see are reasons to be discouraged, fill my mind with all the reasons to praise You—they are countless! When I'm surrounded by a world without hope, open my mouth to share the good news of everlasting hope. Amen.

Hope is always available, but it isn't automatic. By *choosing* to remember who our God is and by *choosing* to offer Him praise, we have hope.

JOY

You followed our way of life and the life of the Lord.
You suffered from others because of listening to us.
But you had the joy that came from the Holy Spirit.
1 THESSALONIANS 1:6 NLV

Lord, living the life You call me to live is not the wide and easy road. It's the opposite! You said that the door is narrow and the road hard that leads to eternal life (Matthew 7:14). And along the way we will suffer for following that hard road. Thank You for the encouragement I need to keep going, Lord. Thank You for the promise that even when walking in obedience means suffering, I have the Holy Spirit's joy—joy that lightens my step, joy that uplifts my spirit, joy that raises my eyes to You. Amen.

Joyful while suffering—the people of the world
may scratch their heads and say that can't be.
But this kind of joy is supernatural. This kind
of joy can come only from on high.

THE DELIVERER

He has delivered us from such a deadly peril,
and he will deliver us again. On him we have set
our hope that he will continue to deliver us.
2 CORINTHIANS 1:10 NIV

Father, Paul knew Your track record of deliverance. He had heard the stories of how You delivered Your people in the past, and he had seen how You delivered him in the present. So he clung to that truth and set his hope on You to deliver in the future too. Your track record of deliverance has not changed over the centuries. You still deliver Your people. You still reach down and pull us out of life's perils, and ultimately You reach down and bring our souls to You. Whether in peril or peace, Father, my hope lies in You. Amen.

Need a reminder of God's track record? The psalmists often recounted the history of God's faithful love and deliverance. Check out Psalm 136 for starters.

GOD PLEASERS

*Am I now trying to win the approval of human beings,
or of God? Or am I trying to please people? If I were still
trying to please people, I would not be a servant of Christ.*
GALATIANS 1:10 NIV

I'm a people pleaser, Lord. And when it comes to living for
You, being a people pleaser is not a good trait. Sometimes I
try to make it sound good. I tell myself that I just care what
people think and how they feel. But if I'm honest, I actually
care what people think *about me*. I want their approval. Lord,
the way I live as a Christian will not always be popular, but
that isn't what matters. I live to please You! As long as I can
look toward You and see Your nod of approval, that is what
matters most. Amen.

There is a difference between seeking people's
approval and seeking people's good. Paul said,
"I want to please everyone in all that I do." Yet don't
skip his motive: "I want to do what is best for them
so they may be saved" (1 Corinthians 10:33 NLV).

DEATH, WHERE IS THY STING?

We do not want you to be uninformed about those who sleep in death, so that you do not grieve like the rest of mankind, who have no hope. For we believe that Jesus died and rose again, and so we believe that God will bring with Jesus those who have fallen asleep in him.
1 Thessalonians 4:13–14 niv

Life and death—one brings great joy; the other, great sorrow. Lord, more and more it's clear that this world that's so full of life is also so full of death. But Your promise is clearer still: a time is coming when You will wipe every tear from our eyes and death will be no more (Revelation 21:4). Jesus died and rose again for us. And though we die, we will live again. Though death claims those we love, we will be brought together again in a world with no mourning, no pain, *no death*. Hasten the day, Lord. Amen.

Now—not later—is the time to tell a grieving world about the one who raises the dead.

WAKE-UP CALL

For you are children of the light and of the day.
We are not of darkness or of night. Keep awake!
Do not sleep like others. Watch and keep your
minds awake to what is happening.
1 Thessalonians 5:5–6 nlv

God, You called me out of darkness into Your truth. You called me Your daughter, and I became a child of the light. Your Son shines on my life so I can see the way to live, but lately I catch myself drifting asleep. I'm not paying as much attention to how I'm living. I'm closing my eyes to what is going on around me. God, draw me from the shadows to the bright day where I belong as a child of the light, a child of the Lord. Help me live awake—with my mind alert, my eyes open, and my heart awaiting You. Amen.

Christ calls us to *live.* So "let's not sleepwalk through life" (1 Thessalonians 5:6 MSG). Let's be on the lookout for the devil's snares. Let's make the most of our time. Let's give it all we've got!

HOLY FIRE

Do not quench the Spirit.
1 THESSALONIANS 5:19 NIV

Holy Spirit, so much of what You do I welcome with open arms. Like the times You comfort me when I am hurting and strengthen me when I am weak. The times You pray the prayers that I can't pray. The times You guide me along difficult paths. But some of what You do I want to push away. Like the times You convict my heart. Then I try to ignore Your presence; I try to quench Your work in me. Spirit, show me where I go wrong. Help me be open to all that You do. Amen.

Patterns of sin can dampen the flame of God's Spirit in believers—making it harder for us to sense Him. The solution? Turn from the sin and return to God. Draw near to Him, and He will draw near to you (James 4:8).

MAY GOD. . .

Now may the God of peace make you holy in every way, and may your whole spirit and soul and body be kept blameless until our Lord Jesus Christ comes again. God will make this happen, for he who calls you is faithful.
1 Thessalonians 5:23–24 NLT

Lord, thank You for these words. Thank You for the reassurance that I'm not on my own to live a godly life. I *try* to be Christlike, and I stumble along. But I fail a lot too. When all my efforts seem like wasted efforts, I'm reminded to rely on the one who called me. Paul prayed that *You* would make the believers holy. He wanted them *to be kept* blameless. God of peace, set me apart for Yourself. Keep me—spirit, soul, and body—blameless until Jesus returns. I will depend on You, for You are ever faithful. Amen.

"The spirit is willing, but the body is weak!" Jesus said. So we must "keep watch *and pray*" (Matthew 26:41 NLT). God can do wonders with a willing spirit if we would only partner with Him.

THE BEST REST

"Come to me, all you who are weary and burdened,
and I will give you rest. Take my yoke upon you. . . .
For my yoke is easy and my burden is light."
MATTHEW 11:28–30 NIV

Lord, my feet are shuffling, my shoulders stooped. Weariness and burdens have been my companions for a while now. I try to lighten the load by relaxing, by sleeping, by de-stressing, and somehow all that effort just makes me more tired! I may look for ways to rest outside of You, Lord, but Your rest is deeper and more complete than any other on this planet. I can come to You weary and burdened, and You ease my soul. You offer a blessedly easy yoke for the wearying one I carry. So I'm coming to You, Lord. Please give me rest. Amen.

On your last leg? Lean on the one who is "gentle and humble in heart" (Matthew 11:29 NIV). Our Lord's presence is a refuge for our worn-out selves.

FULLY EQUIPPED

Then the LORD asked Moses, "Who makes a person's mouth? Who decides whether people speak or do not speak, hear or do not hear, see or do not see? Is it not I, the LORD?"
EXODUS 4:11 NLT

Lord, I understand how Moses felt. You had asked him to go and speak to Pharaoh—a daunting assignment on its own—but Moses wasn't a good speaker. He didn't think he could say eloquently enough what had to be said. Then You pointed to Yourself. *You* made Moses' mouth. *You* give people the ability to speak, hear, see—to do anything! Lord, I need Your words as much as Moses did. Your plans for me might challenge me and stretch me. But then I will look to You—the one who made me and will make me ready for what's ahead. Amen.

Think about it: if God wants us to fulfill
His purposes for us (He does!), then will
He not equip us to do just that?

CALLED TO FORGIVE

*Be kind and compassionate to one another,
forgiving each other, just as in Christ God forgave you.*
Ephesians 4:32 niv

God, I need to forgive someone, but I'm finding forgiveness difficult. I don't want to look past the wrong and let it go, even though that's exactly what You would have me do. You want me to be kind, compassionate, *forgiving*—because that is what You are toward me. God, when I think of how much You've forgiven, all the wrongs You've looked past and made right in my life, I'm awed and I'm humbled. I'm far from deserving forgiveness; You forgive anyway. Thank You for Your forgiveness, God. Help me be as forgiving. Only through You can I be like You. Amen.

Peter asked, "Should I forgive someone seven times?"
Jesus answered, "Not seven, but seventy times seven"
(Matthew 18:21–22). Translation: umpteen times.
God's forgiveness is immense! We display a sliver of
that forgiveness by forgiving again and again. . .and again.

SHORT MEMORY

The disciples replied, "Where would we get enough food here in the wilderness for such a huge crowd?"
MATTHEW 15:33 NLT

Jesus, You didn't want to send the crowd away hungry; You wanted to feed them first. The disciples looked around at where they were—a remote, barren place—and wondered where the food would come from. How could they forget that You fed five thousand hungry mouths with only five loaves and two fish? But I do that too—I forget that You perform miracles. Lord, I'm looking around at the places in my life that seem remote and barren, and I think they will always be that way. Help me have faith that You work miraculously. Amen.

God does not ask us to believe without evidence.
He has shown us who He is countless times—from
parting the Red Sea to walking on the Sea of Galilee,
from creation to the cross and beyond. How can we forget?

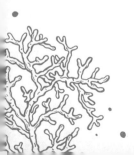

WHAT DO YOU MEAN?

Nicodemus said to Him, "How can a man be born when he is old? How can he get into his mother's body and be born the second time?"
JOHN 3:4 NLV

Lord, You told Nicodemus that unless a person is born again, he or she cannot see the kingdom of God (John 3:3). Nicodemus missed the point. He was thinking about a physical birth when You were talking about a spiritual birth. It's easy to catch on to that, sitting here reading the verses. But I wonder if I would have understood any better. My mind is so often fastened on earthly things. I don't think in terms of God all the time. Lord, help me think spiritually. Open my mind to what You are teaching me through Your Word and my life. Amen.

Nicodemus heard "born again" and thought of a womb. The disciples heard Jesus say "yeast of the Pharisees" and thought of bread (Matthew 16:6–7). We humans don't always get it, but we have God to help us understand.

IN HIM

*"I have told you these things so you may have peace
in Me. In the world you will have much trouble.
But take hope! I have power over the world!"*
JOHN 16:33 NLV

Lord, You said it, and I see it every day—*in this world I will
have much trouble.* I don't need to be convinced of the truth
of Your words. So why do I sometimes doubt the truth of Your
promise of peace? If I'm peace-less, it's because I'm not going
to the source of peace. In this world I have troubles, but *in
You* I have peace. When the troubles of my world crowd out
peace, Lord, may I seek peace in You, the one who has power
over every trouble, over the entire world. Thank You for the
peace I find in You. Amen.

As a temporary resident of the world, you have a
guarantee of trouble. But take hope! Jesus has already
overcome the world. And His peace is a guarantee too.

A PRAYER FOR DELIVERANCE

Pray that we may be delivered from wicked and evil people,
for not everyone has faith. But the Lord is faithful, and he
will strengthen you and protect you from the evil one.
2 THESSALONIANS 3:2–3 NIV

Lord, Christians here at home and all around the world encounter persecution and harm from unbelievers. Centuries ago, Christians were experiencing the same thing. That's why Paul asked believers to pray for deliverance from the actions of wicked and evil people. "Not everyone has faith," he wrote. But before those inked words had a chance to dry, he pointed out that *You are faithful.* You would strengthen and protect. Lord, today I pray for Christians wherever they are, wherever they need delivering from evil. Give them strength through Your Spirit. Shield them with Your wings. Amen.

The evil one may seem to have the upper hand
in our world, but he does not. Evil may abound
momentarily, but God prevails eternally.

FOR GOODNESS' SAKE

Let us not become weary in doing good, for at the proper
time we will reap a harvest if we do not give up.
GALATIANS 6:9 NIV

Lord, I try to follow Your blueprint for life because I know that
Your every word is spoken with my welfare in mind. I try to
serve others—to do the good works You call me to. But some
days it seems as if there's no point to living righteously and
lovingly, as if "doing good" is in vain because all the good just
evaporates. Upend that mindset, Lord, for it is not from You.
Renew my energy to persevere, for You have promised that
I will reap a harvest if I do not give up. Let me not become
weary of doing good. Amen.

When doing good seems to do no good, think on God—
of His goodness that He pours out on us,
and of His greatness to make all things work
together for good (Romans 8:28).

GIFTS GALORE

*God has given each of you a gift. Use it to help
each other. This will show God's loving-favor.*
1 PETER 4:10 NLV

God, Your children are gifted! You give each one of us a gift that is all our own, and through Your gifting we can do amazing, inspiring things. In our humanness we sometimes make these gifts about us. I'm guilty of that. I want to use my gift to enrich my life and to feel good about myself. But Your gifts aren't about the giftee. They are meant to be shared. They are meant to show who *You* are. God, teach me how to use my gift as You intended. Help me seek the joy of giving from the gift I've been given. Amen.

Some gifts are obvious, some subtle. Maybe you don't know what your gift is. Or maybe you don't know how to use your gift to serve God and others. Talk to the giver.

NEVER OUT OF STOCK

God is able to bless you abundantly, so that in all things at all times, having all that you need, you will abound in every good work.

2 Corinthians 9:8 niv

God, I love the lavishness of this promise. You aren't just able to bless sparingly, with a sprinkle here, a sprinkle there. You are able to bless *abundantly*. Your storehouses are packed to the rafters, ready to supply us with whatever we need—in all things, at all times—for every good work. God, I hate to admit it, but my heart isn't always as generous as Your promise. I want to hold on to my blessings; I don't trust that You will refill what I empty out. But I can never ever give away more than You are able to provide. Amen.

God isn't kidding about blessing our giving. And He wants to prove it: "I will open the windows of heaven for you. I will pour out a blessing so great you won't have enough room to take it in! Try it! Put me to the test!" (Malachi 3:10 nlt).

FEEL FREE TO SHARE

You have searched me, Lord, and you know me.
You know when I sit and when I rise; you perceive my
thoughts from afar. You discern my going out and my
lying down; you are familiar with all my ways.
PSALM 139:1–3 NIV

Lord, sometimes I shy away from prayer. I might be ashamed because I've sinned and would rather hide from You. Or I might think that my prayers are silly. But Lord, You already know what's on my heart—You know absolutely everything about me. You know my comings and goings. You know my thoughts. You know my ways. Nothing I say to You will surprise You. Nothing I share with You will shock You. Nothing I pray will change how You feel about me. *Nothing* will subtract one bit of Your vast love. Help me open up to You, Lord. Amen.

We might think, *If God knows everything, why pray?*
Prayer doesn't clue God in, that's for sure. But
prayer does deepen our relationship with Him.

DECEITFUL HEARTS

*The heart is deceitful above all things,
and desperately sick; who can understand it?*
JEREMIAH 17:9 ESV

Lord, as much as I'd like to think I understand my heart, I don't. As much as I'd like to think my heart is all good, it's actually desperately sick. Oh Lord, I need You so! This side of heaven, I will never be able to understand the hidden spaces of my heart. But You search my heart. You understand it. And Lord, only You can heal it. Please remove the rotten, sinful parts so that what You find inside is pleasing in Your eyes. Lord, make my heart new! And each day, shed Your light where my heart would deceive me. Amen.

"The human heart is. . .desperately wicked. Who really knows how bad it is?" (Jeremiah 17:9 NLT). What a hard truth to swallow! But what a picture of God's amazing grace that He would choose to look on us with love.

IMMEASURABLY MORE

Now to him who is able to do immeasurably
more than all we ask or imagine, according
to his power that is at work within us.
EPHESIANS 3:20 NIV

Lord, once again I'm reminded of Your amazing ability. When I pray to You, I don't have to wonder if You can do what I ask, what I imagine. You can do immeasurably more! I may think I'm asking for something huge. I may think I'm imagining something impossible. But Your view is so much wider than mine. Your vision is so much broader. Your plans are so much bigger. Your power is so much greater, and it's that power that makes immeasurably more a reality. Lord, thank You for working amazingly in me. To You be the glory. Amen.

The power at work in us today is the same power that raised Christ from the dead. *Believe* that God is able to do much, much more than all you ask or imagine!

PRAY, PRAY, PRAY

Pray continually. . .for this is
God's will for you in Christ Jesus.
1 THESSALONIANS 5:17–18 NIV

God, prayer is a lifestyle. Or at least, it should be. Communicating with You should be woven into my life so that it touches everything I do; but many times, prayer is just an isolated part of my day. It's a few words in the morning before I head out the door or a few words in the evening as I wind down. It's a nod of acknowledgment in Your direction as I go about my day on my own. God, help me make Your will my desire. Help me pray continually. Keep me praying even when difficulties discourage me—help me pray all the more. Amen.

The biblical command to "pray without ceasing"
(1 Thessalonians 5:17 KJV) doesn't mean
never stopping to take a breath. It does mean
praying regularly and without giving up.

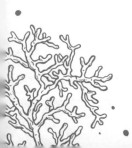

AS SIMPLE AS THAT

"Ask, and it will be given to you; seek, and you will find; knock, and it will be opened to you."
MATTHEW 7:7 ESV

Lord, prayer is not Your concession to me. You tell me to come to You! You are not a reluctant hearer of my prayers. You want me to talk with You! You say to ask, to seek, to knock. Lord, why do I ever hesitate to pray? Why do I keep my prayers bottled up inside? Why do I try to make complex what You have made beautifully simple? Like a daughter running to her father's side and looking up, brimming with words, I can run to You, asking, seeking, knocking. And if that wasn't enough, Lord, You promise to answer me. Amen.

Jesus' model prayer (Matthew 6:9–13) demonstrates that prayer doesn't have to be complicated. Prayer is, after all, just a conversation between child and Father.

SURE PRAYERS

*This is the confidence we have in approaching God:
that if we ask anything according to his will, he hears
us. And if we know that he hears us—whatever we
ask—we know that we have what we asked of him.*
1 JOHN 5:14–15 NIV

God, as I look up at You and pray, I long for the confidence that I read about in these verses. But I get hung up on that phrase—"according to his will." God, how can I know Your will? Your thoughts and ways are higher than my own thoughts and ways. A lot of the time, I believe Your will is a mystery. But I *can* know Your will, God. The more I read Your Word, the more I know You. Each moment I spend with You in prayer attunes my heart to Yours. May all that I ask be according to Your will! Amen.

God is working in our lives. As we yield to Him,
His desires become our desires, and praying according
to His will becomes as natural as breathing.

COMFORTED

*Praise be to. . .the Father of compassion and the God
of all comfort, who comforts us in all our troubles,
so that we can comfort those in any trouble with
the comfort we ourselves receive from God.*
2 CORINTHIANS 1:3–4 NIV

Father of compassion, God of all comfort, I need Your comfort today. I'm hurting, and the hurt won't let up. I've cried and cried, but still the tears flow. Replace the hurt with Your hope. Dry the tears with Your love. Surround me with Your presence so that I know I'm not alone. Even now, just being near You in prayer, I feel Your comfort. I'm able to lift my voice in praise of You, the one who reigns over the universe yet holds me close. And when this trouble passes, God, use me to comfort others as You are comforting me. Amen.

Seeing how we are comforted during our troubles
may be just what someone needs to look up
and see the God who did the comforting.

CLOCK OUT!

*It is useless for you to work so hard from early
morning until late at night, anxiously working
for food to eat; for God gives rest to his loved ones.*
PSALM 127:2 NLT

Lord, considering all the ease our modern life gives us, we humans still work like dogs! We toil through long work-weeks and weekend work, with hardly any sleep. I've gotten caught in the endless work cycle before, especially when I'm worrying about the future. I question whether I'll have enough money for what I need, so I work harder, hoping for security. Lord, help me to put aside my striving and rely on You, for You promise to take care of me. Help me to put on hold the next day's work and sleep soundly, for You give me rest. Amen.

Where is the line between "hard worker"
and "workaholic"? Ask God to help you set
limits on work. Then, when you have done
your part, trust God to provide the rest.

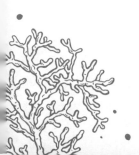

SPIRIT-TAUGHT

You have received the Holy Spirit, and he lives within you,
so you don't need anyone to teach you what is true.
For the Spirit teaches you everything you need to know.
1 John 2:27 nlt

Holy Spirit, the more years I live, the more I realize that navigating life isn't as easy as following a map. Every day I make decisions, some so minor that I don't even realize I'm making a choice. And every day I hear and read conflicting ideas of what is true. Help me look within to know what is truly true. You are there, teaching me, guiding me. Help me be open to Your leading. Today I commit to spending time in prayer. As I pray, draw my spirit so close to Yours that I hear Your messages loud and clear. Amen.

John's statement "You don't need anyone to teach you" does not discount the value of our pastors and Bible teachers. But even without them around, God is able to teach us all things.

FORGIVENESS FOR SINNERS

But God demonstrates his own love for us in this:
While we were still sinners, Christ died for us.
ROMANS 5:8 NIV

God, after I sin, I feel unworthy to come to You. I doubt that You could love me as I am. I try to fix myself up first, thinking *then* I'll pray. And all the while You're saying, *"Come to Me"*—just as You called me before I knew Your name and my need. You didn't wait until I was worthy to love me. You didn't even wait until I was "good enough." You sent Your love to earth while I was still a sinner—while I was Your enemy, Your Son died for me! For that I am eternally grateful. Amen.

God offered forgiveness when we deserved
damnation; He offered life when we deserved
death. The offer still stands! If we confess,
God is faithful to forgive (1 John 1:9).

95

AS A FATHER

The Lord has loving-pity on those who fear Him, as a father has loving-pity on his children. For He knows what we are made of. He remembers that we are dust.
PSALM 103:13–14 NLV

God, what a relief that You don't look down from heaven, see me struggling, and look away in indifference. You understand that I'm only human, because You made every fiber of my being. You're aware of my frailties—how my strength runs out, how I'm prone to sin. You know all my weaknesses, and You have loving-pity on me. You have compassion on me, Your daughter, just like a father. What other god is like You? What other god not only creates but cares? Only You. God, I praise You and I thank You. Amen.

We never have to feel uneasy about approaching God—even when we are at our worst, even in our messiest, ugliest, most miserable state— for almighty God is also our heavenly Father.

GIVE THANKS

*Let them give thanks to the Lord for His loving-kindness
and His great works to the children of men! For He fills the
thirsty soul. And He fills the hungry soul with good things.*
PSALM 107:8–9 NLV

Lord, I don't thank You nearly enough for Your loving-kindness.
I don't thank You nearly enough for the wonderful things You
do. When I think of where and what I would be without You,
well, I don't like to think of it at all. Lord, I'm so glad You've
chosen me to be Your child. You are so good to me! My parched
soul—once dry and cracked like a desert—is drenched in Your
life. My hungry soul—once starved and aching—is satisfied
with Your goodness. For the thousands upon thousands of
reasons to give thanks to You, Lord, I thank You. Amen.

A thankful heart can add color to gray days.
Even in the darkest day, there is *always* something
to thank God for. So let us give thanks!

CRIES FOR HELP

*"LORD, help!" they cried in their trouble,
and he rescued them from their distress.*
PSALM 107:6 NLT

A simple prayer, Lord, is all it takes for You to rescue me. I might be wandering far away. *Lord, help!* And You pull me close and guide my steps. I might be trapped in darkness. *Lord, help!* And You bring light and freedom. I might be suffering because of sin. *Lord, help!* And You forgive me and make me new. I might be struggling through stormy situations. *Lord, help!* And You still the storms and see me to safety. Thank You, Lord, that with just one cry from me to You, You deliver me from my distress. Amen.

God's rescue plans don't all look the same. Sometimes He takes us out of the distress; sometimes He upholds us as we walk through it. But we can count on Him to hear us and to deliver us.

PERFECT TIMING

"For if you keep quiet at this time, help will come to the Jews from another place. But you and your father's house will be destroyed. Who knows if you have not become queen for such a time as this?"
ESTHER 4:14 NLV

God, Esther didn't have a divine revelation from You that told her what was going to happen and why. She had to live each day as it came. But she had courage to risk her life to save the lives of her people. She *was* queen for exactly that time. My life isn't an accident either. When I was born, where I was born, the events I go through—they have a specific purpose because *I* have a specific purpose. God, help me realize Your plans for me. And when I can't see You behind the scenes, help me trust that You are there. Amen.

Although God isn't mentioned in the book of Esther, His presence is evident. God may feel distant in our lives, but He is still near.

CREATED FOR GOOD

For we are God's handiwork, created in
Christ Jesus to do good works, which God
prepared in advance for us to do.
EPHESIANS 2:10 NIV

God, I am Your unique creation. You created each cell in my body and knit them together before I was born. I am the work of Your hands. You chose and formed everything that makes me *me*—from my eye color to my height to my smile. But in making me, You weren't finished once You created my physical being. You thought ahead to my good works. God, as I pray, prepare me for the good works that You have already gotten ready for me. Then, each day, give me eyes to see what You would have me do. Amen.

God has good plans for us as His children, and those good plans include good works. In fact, the best of His good plans stem from the good things we do for others.

100

A TIME FOR EVERYTHING

For everything there is a season,
a time for every activity under heaven.
ECCLESIASTES 3:1 NLT

"For everything there is a season." Lord, we experience so many things in this life, both happy times and hard times—times of planting and uprooting, times of weeping and laughing, times of hurting and healing, times of grieving and dancing. I wish I could skip the bad seasons, but I can't. They are as much a part of my life as the good seasons. Lord, with Your help, I can be patient through the rough patches. I will cry out to You in the bad—but then I will rejoice with You in the good. And in every season, I will pray. Amen.

Looking up in prayer to God is never out of season!
He is our help and hope in every season, whether a
season of joy, sorrow, or somewhere in between.

NOT UNNOTICED

God knows how I work for Him. He knows how I preach with all my heart the Good News about His Son. . . . I pray that I might be able to visit you, if God wants me to.

ROMANS 1:9–10 NLV

God, many times my good works seem to go unseen. All the hours, all the thought and care, all the sacrifice—I give my all, but then it's as if I haven't done anything at all. No one notices. But even if people don't see, You never miss one thing I do to serve You. Like Paul, I can say that You know the ways I work for You. And the fact that You know is all that matters. God, I prayerfully leave my plans with You today and every day. Clear the way for what You want me to do. Amen.

Because we're not working for applause but for God, our good works require zero effort to be noticed—and that frees up 100 percent of our energy to serve the one who does notice.

BY FAITH

The Good News tells us we are made right
with God by faith in Him. Then, by faith
we live that new life through Him.
ROMANS 1:17 NLV

God, thank You for the good news that I am made right with You simply by faith, by believing in Your Son. That good news is the *best* news I will ever receive! Thank You for so great a love that covers all my sins. Now, God, just as I looked to You to make me right—to take me from rebellion to obedience, from condemnation to being Your child—I will continue to look to You to live this life of faith. You saved my life, and You infuse me with life. Through You, next to You, I am alive and well! Amen.

God's plan was never to redeem us and then leave us to our own devices. He wants a restored relationship. He wants to be part of our lives, not just the source.

BETTER THAN

*God's plan looked foolish to men, but it is wiser than
the best plans of men. God's plan which may look
weak is stronger than the strongest plans of men.*
1 Corinthians 1:25 nlv

God, Your thoughts are not our thoughts; Your ways are not our ways. In Your economy, poor equals rich, weak equals strong, foolish equals wise. The world may call us Christians crazy for following a God like You, a God who turns our way of thinking, our way of doing things, on its head—a God who chose a lowly stable birth and a humiliating death as the channel for the greatest love and power we will ever know. God, I believe that Your plan is wiser, that Your plan is stronger—that Your plan is supreme. To it I look. On it I depend. Amen.

God's promised Messiah and His grand plan of salvation weren't what people expected. Likewise, God's plans for our lives may not match our expectations. No matter! Even His most unbelievable plans surpass ours by far.

A CAUSE FOR BOASTING

*But far be it from me to boast except in the cross
of our Lord Jesus Christ, by which the world has
been crucified to me, and I to the world.*
GALATIANS 6:14 ESV

Lord, some Jews in Paul's day boasted about the things they
did to appear religious on the outside. Paul said he would
boast only about the cross and the one who had changed
him from the inside out. In my humanity, I want to get credit
for the good things I do. But my real reason for boasting is
You, Lord. Without You, I could do nothing worth bragging
about anyway! Help me live "crucified" to the world. What
the world values? What the world calls important? That isn't
what I live for, what I rejoice in, what I boast about—but
You are! Amen.

We can spend a lifetime learning what it means
to be crucified with Christ (Galatians 2:20). Then
again, that's precisely what we're intended to
do: spend our lives learning to follow Him.

ON PURITY

Do you not know that your body is a house of God where the Holy Spirit lives? . . . God bought you with a great price. So honor God with your body. You belong to Him.
1 Corinthians 6:19–20 nlv

God, Your message regarding purity isn't the message the world sends. The world says to do what feels good. The world says that my body is my own and that no one has the right to tell me what to do with my body but me. But my body isn't mine, not really. You made me Yours. You converted a shack into a dwelling place for Your Holy Spirit. God, transform my heart from one that desires pleasure to one that seeks to honor You. And when I'm tempted, remind me that Your standards aren't meant to burden me—they're meant to bless me! Amen.

The world's anything-goes attitude toward sex can easily make us question God's commands. Being too close to our culture blurs the line. But drawing close to God makes the truth crystal clear.

UNWELCOME SIN

*I do not understand myself. I want to do what
is right but I do not do it. Instead, I do the very
thing I hate. . . . There is no happiness in me!
Who can set me free from my sinful old self?*
ROMANS 7:15, 24 NLV

Lord, how I wish these verses weren't true of my life! But they are. How I wish I didn't sin! But I do. Deep down I want to obey You. It has never been my aim to disobey. And still I do what is wrong—I do the thing I hate! I throw up my hands, frustrated with failing, and wonder if I'll ever change. Lord, even when I fail again and again, I can turn to You again and again. Thank You for forgiveness, for taking my despair and giving me hope. *You* are the one who can free me! Amen.

"I find it to be a law that when I want to do right, evil
lies close at hand" (Romans 7:21 ESV). Sound familiar?
The devil is ever ready to trip us up as we try to do
right. But God won't ever let us fall completely!

ALL ONE

God does not see you as a Jew or as a Greek. He does not see you as a servant or as a person free to work. He does not see you as a man or as a woman. You are all one in Christ.
GALATIANS 3:28 NLV

God, our world is so quick to label people. Sometimes the labels just describe something about us—gender, ethnicity, age, marital status. . . But sometimes we're judged based on our labels, and that judgment isn't always positive. People put other people down just because they're women or a different race or a lower class. Even in smaller ways, God, it's easy to feel lesser than someone else. But that's a feeling I never have to worry about with You. You don't play favorites. You don't see us as this or that—You see us as Your children, beloved and equal in Christ. Amen.

God created us uniquely, with differences that
define our paths through life. But whoever we are,
we all stand on level ground in God's presence.

WHATSOEVER YOU DO

*And whatever you do, whether in word or deed,
do it all in the name of the Lord Jesus, giving
thanks to God the Father through him.*
Colossians 3:17 niv

Lord, in my everyday tasks, You don't enter my thoughts much—I might not think about You at all. Other times I do. When I'm reading my Bible, when I'm at church, when I have a tough decision to make, when I'm worrying over something—then my mind goes to You. But Lord, You are with me even in the mundane. Everything I do matters to You. Your Word says that *whatever* I do, I should do it in Your name. Help me to be conscious of You with each word, with each deed. Help me to be thankful in each moment. Amen.

For Brother Lawrence, a seventeenth-century Carmelite monk, commonplace things could be holy. Even washing dishes could be an act of worship and time spent in God's presence.

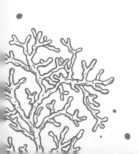

HEALING TOUCH

Just then a woman who had suffered for twelve years with constant bleeding came up behind him. She touched the fringe of his robe, for she thought, "If I can just touch his robe, I will be healed."
MATTHEW 9:20–21 NLT

Lord, this unnamed woman believed that You were so powerful that just to touch the edge of Your garment was enough to heal her. You, being God, didn't need to ask her what she wanted. You turned and said, "Take heart!" You called her Your daughter and told her that her faith had made her well (Matthew 9:22 NIV). Lord, I've been hurting for many years now too. May I be as faith-filled as I come to You with my ailment. May I believe that You are able to comfort and to heal—that just to be near You is enough. Amen.

Praise the Lord! He forgives our sins and heals our diseases; He redeems our lives and crowns us with compassion (Psalm 103:2–4). And we never need an appointment to meet with Him, our great physician.

AS A SHEPHERD

"I am the good shepherd; I know my sheep and my sheep know me—just as the Father knows me and I know the Father—and I lay down my life for the sheep."
JOHN 10:14–15 NIV

Jesus, You care for me like a shepherd who tends his flock. The shepherd watches out for predators that would harm the sheep; You watch over me and guard me from evil. The shepherd leads the sheep to pasture; You guide me through life. The shepherd brings the sheep back when they stray; You gently draw me to Your side when I wander. The shepherd calls to his sheep and they hear; You call me by name and I say, "Here I am." But unlike any other shepherd, Lord, You laid down Your life for me. Thank You, Good Shepherd. Amen.

You're not just "one of the fold" to God. He knows each of His sheep individually—as personally as the Father knows the Son. And He wants us to get to know Him that well too.

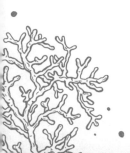

111

STORM SHELTER

God is our safe place and our strength. He is always our help when we are in trouble. So we will not be afraid, even if the earth is shaken and the mountains fall into the center of the sea.
PSALM 46:1–2 NLV

God, it seems the earth is as restless and broken as we are. Storms rage over land and sea as if the wind and rain are crying out. Earthquakes shake the ground as if the land is trembling and falling apart. And those storms stir up anxiety in our hearts. The earthquakes shake us to our very core. We fear the fire and the flood. But even in the middle of unimaginable natural disasters, God, You are our refuge. When I run for shelter from the elements, I will also run to You—my safe place, my help, my reason not to be afraid. Amen.

Natural disasters damage more than roofs. They damage lives. Fear is inevitable—unless we shift our eyes from the clouds to the Son. There we find a center of calm to weather any storm.

JUST WAIT

I did not give up waiting for the Lord. And He turned to me and heard my cry. He brought me up out of the hole of danger, out of the mud and clay. . . . He put a new song in my mouth, a song of praise to our God.
PSALM 40:1–3 NLV

Lord, I'm feeling stuck. I want this situation I'm in to change, but I open my eyes each morning and am greeted by the same old scene. Oh Lord, I need a steady stream of hope, of stamina, of patience to keep waiting for You to move on my behalf. I will keep praying, because I know You will turn to me and hear me. You will pull me from this boggy place where my feet are held. And You will put a new song in my mouth. You will make these cries of discouragement into songs of praise to You! Amen.

The Bible has many verses about waiting for the Lord. Coincidence? No. Waiting is part and parcel of the Christian experience, for God's best work in us often comes before His answers.

JOY TO COME

For his anger lasts only a moment, but his favor lasts a lifetime! Weeping may last through the night, but joy comes with the morning.
Psalm 30:5 nlt

Lord, when difficult times—times of grief or trouble or chastening—move in, they seem here to stay. They unpack their bags and settle in inside my heart. But no matter how permanent they *seem*, I know that difficult times will pass. I've seen it in my life before. I'll see it again. The night may be long; the night may be very long indeed. But even a night drowning in tears will be replaced by sweet joy. The sorrow ends with the breaking of a new day. Your favor shines through once more, and Your favor, Lord, lasts forever. Amen.

Like a soft glowing night light, God is with us through the long nights of weeping. Look for reminders of His presence, and anticipate the joy that will come with the morning.

TEARS UPON TEARS

I am tired of crying inside myself. All night long my pillow is wet with tears. I flood my bed with them.
PSALM 6:6 NLV

Lord, for whatever reason, You have allowed me to remain in a place of pain. I'm not the first to experience this. The psalmist flooded his bed with tears. He was worn out from his crying. So, like he did, I turn to You in my pain. I seek You as I lie here this night, staring at the ceiling, eyes heavy with tears and not with sleep. You haven't let one tear fall unseen. You collect all my tears in Your bottle (Psalm 56:8). My pain is precious to You—You don't take it lightly. Maybe You even cry with me. Lord, please bring relief. Amen.

In the dark of night, we are perhaps most susceptible to imagining that God has abandoned us. Reach out to Him even more determinedly. God isn't far away in our pain. He is near to the brokenhearted (Psalm 34:18).

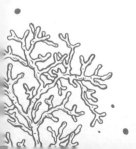

115

NOT DEFEATED

We are afflicted in every way, but not crushed;
perplexed, but not driven to despair; persecuted,
but not forsaken; struck down, but not destroyed.
2 Corinthians 4:8–9 esv

God, Your people have gone through tremendously hard circumstances. We each have our own share of hardship. But even when we are brought to our lowest point, we are never there for good. We may be afflicted, but we are not crushed. We may be perplexed, but we do not despair. We may be persecuted, but we are not left alone. We may be struck down, but we will rise again. And that's all because of You, God. You uphold us. You actually build us up through difficulties if we yield ourselves to You. God, You bring victories from defeats! Amen.

As the stone was rolled in front of Jesus' tomb, it must have looked like a crushing defeat to the disciples. But in three days' time, Jesus would crush death.

A FRIEND IN BETRAYAL

Even my close friend in whom I trusted, who ate
my bread, has lifted his heel against me.
But you, O LORD, be gracious to me.

PSALM 41:9–10 ESV

Lord, a friend I thought I knew has done what I never would have thought possible of her. She has always been so loyal. I could always put my trust in her. But now she has turned against me. My friend has become an enemy. Oh, why do friends betray us? David was betrayed. Jesus, You were betrayed. You knew the sting of a friend turning his back on You. So I'm praying to You today, knowing You will understand, knowing that even if every friend betrays me, You are faithful, You are trustworthy, You are my friend. And You will always be so. Amen.

Humans will let us down. (*We* will let others
down too.) But when we feel let down, we can
look up. God will not let us down, not ever.

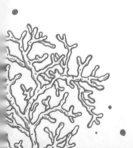

CONSIDER THE HEAVENS

When I consider your heavens, the work of your fingers, the moon and the stars, which you have set in place, what is mankind that you are mindful of them, human beings that you care for them?
<small>PSALM 8:3–4 NIV</small>

God, I look up into the sky tonight, and I'm amazed by the magnificence of Your creation—the billions of stars strewn across the sky, but each named and hung in their place; the soft glow of the moon that gives light even in darkness. That You thought to create such a universe is far beyond me. As vast as the heavens are, You are vaster! You hover over the universe. You hold everything together. And yet You live in me. You know me through and through. More amazing still, You think about me and care for me. What an amazing God You are! Amen.

The universe is a masterful creation by God. But His masterpiece isn't the Milky Way or any other celestial body. It's human beings made in the image of the Master.

THEN AND NOW

*"The LORD who rescued me from the paw of
the lion and the paw of the bear will rescue
me from the hand of this Philistine."*
1 SAMUEL 17:37 NIV

Lord, David took on a formidable foe when he said he'd fight Goliath. There David stood, shepherd boy versus seasoned warrior, with just a slingshot for a weapon. But David's shield was You, Lord. When he needed courage to face a giant, he looked back to how You, his God, had helped him before. Just as You saved David from the lion and the bear, so You would save him from the Philistine. Lord, You have been with me through many challenges. I can look back and see how You helped me then, and I can look forward and know You will help me again. Amen.

God didn't throw David in at the deep end. He had increased David's courage over time until the time came for David to face Goliath. Through our small challenges, God may be preparing us for something bigger.

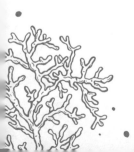

119

ASKING AMISS

You do not get things because you do not ask
for them. Or if you do ask, you do not receive
because your reasons for asking are wrong.
You want these things only to please yourselves.
JAMES 4:2–3 NLV

Lord, how many of my prayers go "unanswered" because I've asked wrongly? I ask You for a lot of things, thinking that my reasons for asking are good reasons—I might even be able to twist my requests around so that it sounds as if I'm not asking for myself but for Your glory. I'm like a little kid who buys her dad a baseball glove for his birthday, guessing that she'll be the one to play with it. Lord, help me pray unselfishly. Help me see beyond my wants to what You want for me. Help me to ask and to ask rightly. Amen.

To keep our prayers from being self-seeking,
we must seek God before self. As our lives revolve
around Him, our prayers will follow suit.

EVERYTHING WE NEED

By his divine power, God has given us everything we
need for living a godly life. We have received all of this by
coming to know him, the one who called us to himself.
2 PETER 1:3 NLT

Lord, a godly life is a life of holiness. Your standards are high, and when I view my life next to those standards, I fall short. Sometimes I begin to believe that I don't have what it takes to live a godly life. But Your Word says that You give me all I need "for holy living" (2 Peter 1:3 NLV). You have been giving me all I need from the very beginning. You called me to Yourself. You let me know who You are. You set me apart and gave me Your Spirit. Lord, help me rely on You alone. Amen.

When we feel our lack, God is our source. Living a godly life is impossible for us, but "what is impossible with man is possible with God" (Luke 18:27 ESV).

UP CLOSE

"Only be very careful to obey the Law which the Lord's servant Moses told you. Love the Lord your God. Walk in all His ways. Obey His Laws. Stay close to Him, and work for Him with all your heart and soul."
JOSHUA 22:5 NLV

Lord, Joshua's parting advice to the eastern tribe included a call to obedience but also to relationship. As they began life after finally taking possession of their land, they needed to follow Your commands, but they also needed to walk alongside You. You wanted them to love You and stay close to You. They were to *cling to You* (Joshua 22:5 ESV). And You want me to do the same. Sometimes I walk at a distance from You. I keep You in sight, but I'm living on my own. Lord, pull me into a closer walk with You and guide me. Amen.

God tells us, "Stay close!" Why? There is safety in nearness. There is also strength, joy, peace, and comfort. There isn't a better place to be than next to our God.

NOT BY OUR MEANS

"And I sent the hornet before you, which drove them out before you, the two kings of the Amorites; it was not by your sword or by your bow."
JOSHUA 24:12 ESV

Lord, You brought Your people into the promised land. And You did it in ways only You could achieve. Still today when met with an obstacle or problem, we humans turn to ourselves first, but You plan events so that we must turn to You. We are tempted to think that we make things happen, but You chart courses so there is no doubt who is God. For all the miracle moments that show Your presence in our lives, Lord, for every time You prepare the way before us, I praise You. I turn to You; I trust in You, my God. Amen.

God gives us good things expecting that we will look to Him. So let's give Him honor and faithfulness in return (Joshua 24:13–14).

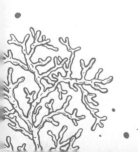

WHAT ABOUT THE WICKED?

*When I tried to understand all this, it troubled
me deeply till I entered the sanctuary of God;
then I understood their final destiny.*
PSALM 73:16–17 NIV

God, the psalmist saw the wicked prospering while the righteous suffered. He couldn't understand why; he was troubled deeply. I look around at our modern world, and nothing has changed. Maybe things have even gotten worse. Wickedness seeps in and causes pain, but the wicked never seem hurt. They go on and on. The psalmist could only understand when he entered Your sanctuary. So, God, I will do that too. I will seek Your presence. I will cry out to You about all that deeply troubles me. And in You I will find reassurance that You won't let the wicked go on forever. Amen.

Evil abounds, *but* "be sure of this: The wicked will not go unpunished" (Proverbs 11:21 NIV); "the light of the wicked will be snuffed out" (Proverbs 13:9 NLT).

BEASTLY BELIEVERS

*I was brutish and ignorant; I was like a beast
toward you. Nevertheless, I am continually
with you; you hold my right hand.*
PSALM 73:22–23 ESV

Lord, at a low point, the psalmist says he was brutish and ignorant and like a beast toward You. All the bitterness and discouragement filling him caused him to lash out. But even then—*nevertheless*—You remained constant. Lord, in times of stress and pain, I sometimes act horribly toward You. I don't want to excuse my bad behavior. I don't want to exploit Your faithfulness. You deserve reverence, Lord. Yet I'm thankful that even when I'm beastly, You choose to bless me with Your presence. Even when my fist is clenched tight in anger, You reach for me and hold my hand. Amen.

All of us have gone astray (Isaiah 53:6)—
rebels against God. But even then, God sent His
Son to die for us so that we could be near Him.

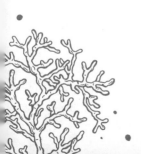

NO ONE AND NOTHING BUT GOD

Whom have I in heaven but You?
I want nothing more on earth, but You.
PSALM 73:25 NLV

God, I depend on all kinds of things and people. I want things too. But the psalmist's words remind me to put every ounce of my hope and trust in You. At the end of the day, You are my greatest desire. When push comes to shove, You are the one on whom I can depend. Nothing in the highest heaven can compare. Nothing on the dusty ground of earth can compare. Whether I look up or look down, God, the eyes of my heart should rest on You. Whom have I in heaven? What could I want on earth? Just You. Amen.

Abundance is mainstream, so Psalm 73:25 might sound radical by narrowing the field to God alone. But the life God calls us to is radically different from the world. And, really, who or what else is above God?

MY STRENGTH AND PORTION

*My health may fail, and my spirit may
grow weak, but God remains the strength
of my heart; he is mine forever.*
PSALM 73:26 NLT

God, I wish it were possible to walk through life without getting bruised physically and emotionally. But in a world that is broken, my body breaks down too. My spirit breaks down. I get sick and weary and worn out. Through all the sickness and weariness and worn-outness, though, You are strength that keeps my hope alive. Though I lose *everything*, I still have You, and I will have You eternally. God, I'm feeling the brokenness of my body today, and I feel my spirit waning. As I sit with You in the stillness, help me tap into the heart strength that flows from You. Amen.

Our flesh fails us, but God will never fail us.
He is our strength and our portion. All we
need to do is lift our eyes to Him.

A DIFFERENT PATTERN

Again the Israelites did evil in the LORD's sight,
so the LORD handed them over to the Philistines.
JUDGES 13:1 NLT

Lord, over and over in the book of Judges the people do what is evil. So You, a righteous God, punish. The people then cry out. And You, a merciful God, deliver. Your patience and faithfulness and mercy astound me, God! I know I can turn to You and cry out for help even in my sin. But Lord, I don't want to see that pattern in my life. I don't want to snub Your commands and go my own way, only to trip and fall headlong into trouble. I'd rather go Your way with my first step and follow You each step after that. Amen.

The true-life stories in the Bible give us comfort for the times we make mistakes. Better yet, they serve as a caution for what *not* to do in the first place.

CUT DOWN TO SIZE

The LORD said to Gideon, "You have too many men.
I cannot deliver Midian into their hands, or Israel would
boast against me, 'My own strength has saved me.' "
JUDGES 7:2 NIV

Father, Gideon and Israel had an enemy to defeat. But as You prepped them for battle, You did what must have seemed irrational (to our human minds, at least). You told Gideon that his army was too big. Twice You reduced the ranks until a mere three hundred men remained. It was clear: Israel couldn't look to themselves for victory—they had to look to You. Father, in my life when resources dwindle, when no solution is in sight, when there is nothing I can do—those are the times when I see You most clearly. Amen.

We may hate feeling small in situations that
aren't in our control. But maybe feeling small is
just what we need to realize how big God is.

AND WE WORSHIP

*As soon as Gideon heard the telling of the dream and
its interpretation, he worshiped. And he returned
to the camp of Israel and said, "Arise, for the LORD
has given the host of Midian into your hand."*
JUDGES 7:15 ESV

God, after paring down Gideon's army, You knew he might
be fearful. So You told him to go to the enemy camp during
the night. There he overheard two men discussing a dream.
The dream's meaning was good news! And right then he
bowed and worshipped You. When You send encouragement
into my life, God, I don't always acknowledge the source. I
may be relieved; I may even be jumping up and down with joy.
But I want my first thoughts to be worshipful ones—
worshipping the one who does so much for me, the one who
encourages me because You know I'll need encouraging.
Amen.

Gideon didn't wait until the fulfillment of the
interpretation to praise God. He praised Him for
the promise of victory. Even when a victory is far off,
we can still worship God for each win along the way.

PRAY BECAUSE

*I love the Lord, because He hears my voice
and my prayers. I will call on Him as long as
I live, because He has turned His ear to me.*
PSALM 116:1–2 NLV

Lord, there are so many reasons to love You. And one of those reasons I often take for granted: You hear my voice. I'm not talking to myself when I talk things over in the morning hours or through the darkest night. My words don't reverberate into nothingness. You hear my prayers. You are God Almighty, yet You listen to what I say. I love You, Lord, because You hear me. You choose to turn Your ear to me, so I will call on You every day of my life, each day You grant me on earth. I will pray as long as I have breath to pray. Amen.

God hears our prayers and we love Him. The feeling is mutual. God loves to hear our prayers: "The Lord hates the gifts of the sinful, but the prayer of the faithful is His joy" (Proverbs 15:8 NLV).

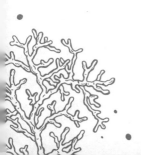

HOW LONG?

How long, O LORD? Will you be angry forever? . . .
But we your people, the sheep of your pasture,
will give thanks to you forever; from generation
to generation we will recount your praise.
PSALM 79:5, 13 ESV

Lord, the psalmist wanted to know "how long." How long would You let the trouble last? How long would Your anger burn? Yet even with "How long?" hanging over Your people, still they would give You thanks. Right now I'm wondering how long. How long, Lord, will this trouble I'm in go on? Why aren't You intervening? Have I angered You for good? I don't know how long, but I will praise You anyway. I will turn to You even in the unknown and give You thanks. I will put my trust in Your timing, however long it takes. Amen.

God values honesty in our lives, and that's no different
in our prayer lives. Sometimes all we can pray are
questions. But always we can rest in God's answers.

ALL OUR WAYS

Seek his will in all you do, and he will
show you which path to take.
PROVERBS 3:6 NLT

Lord, You don't want me to seek Your will in some things but not others. You don't want me to seek Your will just in the major and not the minor. You want me to seek Your will in everything I do. You want me to acknowledge You in all my ways. Then, Lord, You will take the winding, crooked paths in front of me and make them straight. You will set me on the right path and lead me as I go. Lord, help me seek Your will—help me seek *You*—constantly. Help me bring every part of my life to You. Amen.

The first half of Proverbs 3:6 can be translated "in all your ways submit to him" (NIV). That word *submit* is key. What's the use of God making our paths straight unless we are willing to follow His path from the start?

PRESENT-TENSE PRAYERS

"Give your entire attention to what God is doing right now, and don't get worked up about what may or may not happen tomorrow. God will help you deal with whatever hard things come up when the time comes."
MATTHEW 6:34 MSG

Lord, I'm worrying about something that's in the future. I'm feeling anxious about an event that is still days away. I'm afraid I won't have enough courage to make it through. I'm afraid I won't have enough strength either. I've been praying for the courage and strength I'll need, but I still feel nervous and weak. I think I know why, though. I *will* need Your strength and courage then, but not now. Now I need assurance that You will supply exactly what I need, the moment I need it. Calm my fretful heart with Your promise to be with me then—as You are now. Amen.

"Do not worry about tomorrow, for tomorrow will worry about itself" (Matthew 6:34 NIV). God gives us *this day* to live (Psalm 118:24). All else can wait till tomorrow.

OTHERWORLDLY PEACE

*"Peace I leave with you. My peace I give to you.
I do not give peace to you as the world gives.
Do not let your hearts be troubled or afraid."*
JOHN 14:27 NLV

Jesus, when Isaiah prophesied Your birth, he said that You would be called Wonderful Counselor, Mighty God, Everlasting Father, and *Prince of Peace* (Isaiah 9:6). Peace Himself was coming to earth. And before You left earth, You promised to leave peace with Your followers, but not a run-of-the-mill peace. Just as You came from outside the world to bring peace, the kind of peace You left would not be of the world. It was Your peace. Jesus, You are not physically here with me, but Your presence is with me. Along with Your presence comes peace. And how I need Your peace today! Amen.

The peace that will buoy us through unsettled times is not a flimsy human peace. We cannot produce this peace ourselves. We must look to the Lord—the Prince of Peace.

EYE TO EYE

*I will instruct thee and teach thee in the way which
thou shalt go: I will guide thee with mine eye.*
PSALM 32:8 KJV

Lord, You don't expect me to know everything about living a
godly life. How could I? Left on my own, I would wander. But
You promise to instruct me, to teach me—to show me how to
live. You promise to guide me with Your eye. With Your eye,
Lord. I have to look at You to see Your eye. I have to face You
to see Your face. I have to seek You for You to fully lead me.
In my times of prayer, Lord, keep my spiritual eyes focused,
not shifting to other thoughts, but locked on You. Amen.

Like children who can't sit still, we may find
it difficult to settle down to pray. Prayer is a
discipline. Prayer takes practice. Becoming a
better prayer happens one prayer at a time.

ALONE TIME— WITH GOD

But Jesus often withdrew to lonely places and prayed.
Luke 5:16 niv

Jesus, with each passing day of Your earthly ministry the crowds grew. As word spread, the multitudes sought You to hear Your teaching and to be healed. I would have been overwhelmed with all those people pressing in, pleading for attention. Maybe Your flesh felt the strain too. You often left the crowds to meet with the Father. I don't have crowds of people following me around. Even so, life itself presses in on me, calling for my attention. Usually I wait for a quiet moment to pray. But You didn't wait—You created the quiet moment. What if I did that too? Amen.

Jesus led by example, and at times He chose prayer over people. He wasn't neglecting His duty or being unloving. He was taking His eyes off the world to look heavenward and spend some time at His Father's knee.

UNFRIEND THE WORLD

Don't you know that friendship with the world means enmity against God?... Or do you think Scripture says without reason that he jealously longs for the spirit he has caused to dwell in us? But he gives us more grace.
JAMES 4:4–6 NIV

God, You've ransomed me with Christ's blood. You've sealed me with Your Spirit. You've told me to put nothing above You and to love You with my entire heart and soul and mind. No wonder You are a jealous God when I'm unfaithful to You. I don't ever want to be Your enemy, God. Yet without even realizing I'm doing it, I make friends with this world. A compromise here, a compromise there, and suddenly I'm not living wholly devoted to You. But You give more grace, more loving-favor! Thank You, God, for the chance to forsake the world and be called Your friend. Amen.

God resists the proud. But to the humble? He shows favor. When we admit our shortcomings, God makes up the difference. When we give ourselves to Him (James 4:7 NLV), He gives us grace to stand.

AGAIN

O God, You are right and good, as the heavens are high. You have done great things, O God. Who is like You? You have shown me many troubles of all kinds. But You will make me strong again. And You will bring me up again from deep in the earth.
PSALM 71:19–20 NLV

God, You don't keep every trouble away from me. You cause me to walk through the bitter as well as the sweet. I may count down the moments until the bitter is over, yearning for a taste of sweetness, but even in the bitterest, there's hope, because You will make me strong again. You will bring me up again, even from the depths. I look up and see Your goodness stretching into the heavens. And I know that in Your faithfulness You will show me Your goodness in my life again. Who is like You, God, and so worthy of praise! Amen.

Don't allow bitter times to sour your heart toward God. True faith says, "I trust," when trusting is hardest. It says, "I have hope," when hope is not yet a glimmer.

KINGLY SIGHT

In those days Israel had no king;
everyone did as they saw fit.
JUDGES 21:25 NIV

Lord, this verse is a somber note. *Everyone did as they saw fit*—they did what was right in their own eyes. People are still doing what is right in their own eyes, and it brings about horrible consequences. *Israel had no king.* People today are without a king; there is no one ruling in their hearts but them. But I have a king—the King of kings. You, Lord. I don't want to do what is right in my eyes. I want to do what is right in Yours. I want to see my life through Your eyes. Lord, grant me Your vision. Amen.

People may do what is right in their own eyes,
but God hasn't lost control. People may
brush God off, but He is still King!

SLUMBER

*I will both lay me down in peace, and sleep:
for thou, LORD, only makest me dwell in safety.*
PSALM 4:8 KJV

Lord, it's early in the morning, hours before dawn, and I can't sleep. My mind is wide awake, my body restless. But instead of letting my thoughts churn, like I usually would, I'll settle my thoughts on You. For You never slumber. You are watching over me—not missing a toss or a turn. You make me lie down in green pastures, head cradled on soft grass, heart at rest in Your care. And because You make me dwell in safety, I can lie down and sleep in peace. Quiet me with Your love. Lord, lay me down to sleep. Amen.

Children cry out to Mom or Dad when awakened in the night. We, God's children, can call on Him—then close our eyes as our Father's presence calms us back to sleep.

THE GOD OF ISRAEL

*"The LORD repay you for what you have done, and a
full reward be given you by the LORD, the God of Israel,
under whose wings you have come to take refuge!"*
RUTH 2:12 ESV

Lord, when Ruth stuck by Naomi, following her back to
Bethlehem, she was choosing You. Naomi's God would be
her God—You would be her God. And even when Ruth sought
protection from Boaz, she was choosing to depend on You.
It was Your wings she would take refuge under. It was You
who would reward her. Lord, I am a sojourner here on earth,
and as I make my way through this land that isn't my own,
may I come to You, the God of Israel, for shelter. May my
devotion to You spill over into my life and make me worthy
of Your blessing. Amen.

Ruth did not sit on her hands when she and Naomi
faced hardship. But she did set her hope on God. Ruth
acted, and then she paused, patiently waiting for God
to work through Boaz, her kinsman-redeemer.

GO TELL

*We will tell the children-to-come the praises of
the Lord, and of His power and the great things
He has done. . . . Then they would put their trust
in God and not forget the works of God.*
PSALM 78:4, 7 NLV

God, why would we want to remain silent about the great
things You do? Your awesomeness fills us with shouts of
praise. What's more, the next generation needs to hear. We
need to tell them about You so they will put their trust in You,
so they will not repeat the mistakes of generations before
who turned from You. Maybe now more than ever, our spirits are fickle, changing with the trends. But now more than
ever, our spirits cry out for want of You. Lord, show me how,
show me when to share You with those who are younger.
Amen.

It might be a group of Sunday schoolers,
a teenage neighbor, a relative on social media—
but if God has nudged you to reach out to the
next generation, He will also give the opportunity.
Pray. Then keep your eyes peeled.

143

NOT MUCH TO ASK

He has shown you, O mortal, what is good. And what does the LORD require of you? To act justly and to love mercy and to walk humbly with your God.
MICAH 6:8 NIV

God, out of love for You, I want to live up to Your expectations for me. Then I get the idea in my head that I should be doing more, that I'm not enough yet. But You have shown me what is good, and what do You actually require of me? Simply to live with fairness and kindness and to walk humbly with You. That last part sticks out to me today. You don't require me to sprint ahead. Your desire isn't for me to always be running to impress You. You ask that I walk beside You, one steady step after another. Let's walk today. Amen.

God says, "I desire steadfast love and not sacrifice"; "I want people to know [Me] instead of giving burnt gifts" (Hosea 6:6 ESV, NLV). Just think: God values *us* over anything we could give Him!

DO YOU SEE IT?

"Forget the former things; do not dwell on the past. See, I am doing a new thing! Now it springs up; do you not perceive it?"
ISAIAH 43:18–19 NIV

Lord, I catch myself looking back a lot. I replay all the mistakes I've made. I think about the *what-if*s and *if-only*s. But You say to forget former things, not to dwell on the past. When I hear "dwell," I think of dwelling, as in taking up residence somewhere. But You don't want me to stay put in the past because You are working in my future. You are doing a new thing, and You want me facing forward, eyes raised, so that I can see it as it takes shape. Thank You for the new thing, Lord, for a future and a hope (Jeremiah 29:11). Amen.

"See! I am doing a new thing." A new thing is coming, and the driving force is God. The new is not dependent on us. God tells us just to watch.

BUT THIS HAPPENED THAT. . .

We were under great pressure, far beyond our ability to endure, so that we despaired of life itself. Indeed, we felt we had received the sentence of death. But this happened that we might not rely on ourselves but on God.
2 CORINTHIANS 1:8–9 NIV

God, I've never been in such an intense situation as these verses describe. So immense was the pressure that Paul said they despaired of life itself! They thought they would die in these troubles. But the pain had a purpose—it caused them to rely on You. I have reached low points in my life, but those low points You used as turning points. Would I turn to You if I didn't feel the unbearable weight of my sin? Would I turn to You if I never felt the water lapping at my chin? God, use *every* moment to turn me to You. Amen.

Experience takes head knowledge and makes it heart knowledge. God is reliable, and that fact is never more evident than when we must rely on Him.

CONSIDER

*Only fear the Lord and be faithful to worship
Him with all your heart. Think of the
great things He has done for you.*
1 SAMUEL 12:24 NLV

Whenever I feel my heart pull away from You, Lord, I will think of the great things You have done for me. Whenever I am tempted to put my trust in earthly things, I will think of the great things You have done for me. Whenever I get too wrapped up in myself and think too little of You, I will think of the great things You have done for me. But to keep me from getting to those "whenevers"—to keep me awed before You, faithful toward You—I will think of the great things You have done for me. I will keep my mind on You, Lord. Amen.

Samuel's parting words to Israel implored them to maintain heart contact with God. How could they do this? By considering all He had done for them. Where their minds went, their hearts would follow.

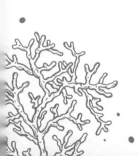

IT'S POSSIBLE!

The disciples were even more amazed, and said to each other, "Who then can be saved?" Jesus looked at them and said, "With man this is impossible, but not with God; all things are possible with God."
MARK 10:26–27 NIV

Lord, You said it's easier for a camel to go through a needle's eye than for the rich to enter the kingdom (Mark 10:25). Your disciples were floored. Who could be saved? How was salvation possible for anyone? But that was Your point, wasn't it? The rich trusted in riches—they had eyes glued on their pocketbooks—when they needed to turn to You. Just so, the disciples were still looking at themselves, but what isn't possible for *us* is possible with *You*. Lord, help me take my eyes off this world so that I can see the impossibilities You make possible. Amen.

Jesus' subject was salvation, but He went further—with Him *all* things are possible. What "impossible" possibility does He want you to see if you would only look up?

148

FOR AND THROUGH

If a man preaches, let him do it with God speaking through him. If a man helps others, let him do it with the strength God gives. So in all things God may be honored through Jesus Christ.
1 PETER 4:11 NLV

God, You would think that the things I do to serve You would be the very things I seek You in first—that I would come to You for the ability to do those good works. But how many times do I plunge ahead in my own strength, without even a prayer to You? Whatever I do *for* You, God, I should do *through* You. If I tell people about You, my words should be the words You give. If I help people, it should be with Your help. May everything I do through You point to You, because then You will be honored. Amen.

We'll know we're walking the right way when what we do circles back to God. For instance, we look to God to serve others, and our service causes others to look to Him.

NO EYE HAS SEEN

The Holy Writings say, "No eye has ever seen or no ear has ever heard or no mind has ever thought of the wonderful things God has made ready for those who love Him."
1 Corinthians 2:9 nlv

God, You are an amazing God! You are far greater than my mind can conceive. I can only begin to grasp Your glory, magnificence, and power. And what You have prepared for me is the work of Your amazing hand. Nothing that I've seen, nothing that I've heard of, nothing that I've imagined comes close. So often I view life with blinders on—only seeing the narrow road ahead of me, unaware of the wide spaces on either side. But You are God of the wide spaces. Your plans unfold without limits, as grand as You can conceive. I await those amazing things, God. Amen.

The devil wants to discourage us with a dismal outlook. But God can brighten the dismal with His promise of the wonderful that He has ready for us.

SUBJECT TO APPROVAL

And David remained in the strongholds
in the wilderness, in the hill country of
the wilderness of Ziph. And Saul sought him
every day, but God did not give him into his hand.
1 SAMUEL 23:14 ESV

God, Saul tried his hardest to find David, searching day in, day out; but You did not give David into Saul's hand. No matter how hard he tried, Saul could not succeed at something You had nixed. The world today is no less evil. People may plan to do us harm, but though they plan, we can relax, trusting that nothing except what You have okayed will happen. God, not one thing catches You unawares, so I don't have to worry. You are in control, so I don't have to be. I am never out of *Your* hand, so I don't have to fear. Amen!

God is your shield, a shield that's impervious to
the terrors of the night and the arrows that
fly by day (Psalm 91:5). Trust Him to protect
you from harm. Trust Him to allow through
only the bad that will be for your good.

LISTEN UP!

"If my people would only listen to me,
if Israel would only follow my ways."
PSALM 81:13 NIV

Lord, throughout the centuries You have said the words you said to ancient Israel: *"If my people would only listen to me."* If Israel would listen to You, then You would subdue their enemies and bless them. But they didn't listen, and You gave them over to their stubbornness. Sadly, surely, You have said it of me too: *"If My daughter would only listen to Me!"* If only I would listen, Lord, in all ways, at all times, what could You then do in my life? Forgive my self-willed ways. Bend my stubborn heart. Open my ears to listen to You. Amen.

In His holiness, God will punish; but in His love, He does not relish the act of punishing. Instead, He calls to us and offers a choice. Oh, if we would only listen to Him!

SOMETHING MORE

He has planted eternity in the human heart,
but even so, people cannot see the whole scope
of God's work from beginning to end.
ECCLESIASTES 3:11 NLT

Lord, is there anyone who hasn't looked at the world as it is and thought, *There has to be more than this*? More than our toil. More than our tears. More than passing pleasures. More than this fleeting life. We feel it in our bones—there has to be more than this! Lord, we feel it in our hearts. You have hardwired us to yearn for something more than this. To look beyond this earth toward eternity. To seek the very one who set eternity inside us, the one who says, *"Yes, there is more than this, and it begins with Me."* Amen.

Humans have tried and failed to get along
without God. Perhaps Augustine said it best:
"You have made us for Yourself, O Lord,
and our heart is restless until it rests in You."

A GODLY WOMAN

A woman who fears the Lord will be praised.
PROVERBS 31:30 NLV

Lord, the pressures on women seem to increase all the time. We get the message that we must be the perfect daughter, sister, wife, mother. If I'm being honest, Proverbs 31 doesn't help. Here is a portrait of a woman who checks all the boxes. She is practically perfect in every way. Who can find a woman like her? Who indeed! But Lord, what makes this woman praiseworthy is her relationship to You. She is a woman of God first; You mold her into her other roles after that. Today I'm putting the pressures aside so I can focus on You and who You are creating me to be. Amen.

The Proverbs 31 woman, in a nutshell: "The fruit of the Spirit is love, joy, peace, forbearance, kindness, goodness, faithfulness, gentleness and self-control" (Galatians 5:22–23 NIV).

IN LOOKING UP

*"In repentance and rest is your salvation,
in quietness and trust is your strength,
but you would have none of it."*
ISAIAH 30:15 NIV

Lord, You see all things, so You see us, Your children, as we try to do things our own way. We try, even though Your way is the only way, even though Your way is so simple. Salvation is in returning to You and resting in You—in leaving behind my sin and leaning on the one who has forgiven and forgotten my sin. Strength is in quietness and trust—in taking a deep breath and turning to my God. Change me, Lord. I don't want to be counted among those who would not look up, but among those who do. Amen.

Maybe in the past we "would have none of it."
Amazingly, despite our rebellion, God "wants to show
[us] kindness. He waits on high to have loving-pity"
(Isaiah 30:18 NLV). What are we waiting for?

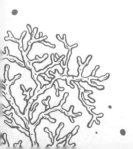

"I HEAR YA!"

He was despised and rejected by mankind,
a man of suffering, and familiar with pain.
ISAIAH 53:3 NIV

Lord, when I pray to You, I am praying to the God of the universe, the God whom the highest heaven cannot contain (1 Kings 8:27). Yet You are not distant. And You are not disconnected. I'm not praying to a God who does not understand. You were a man of suffering; You knew what it is to hurt. You were bruised by life, and You bled. Lord, when I pray to You, I am praying to a confidant—one I can share the pain I've never voiced as I walk through life, knowing You have walked through life before. Lord, hear me as I pray. Amen.

Our Lord comprehends our sorrows. But that's not all.
"Surely he took up our pain and bore our suffering"
(Isaiah 53:4 NIV). God nailed our sorrows to the cross
so we could have a future with no more sorrows.

THIS IS THE DAY

This is the day which the LORD hath made;
we will rejoice and be glad in it.
PSALM 118:24 KJV

God, I've got a lot going on right now. A lot is weighing on my mind. I'm tempted to be glum, waiting for a future time to be glad. I'm tempted to put off rejoicing until another, more joyous day. In heaven we will celebrate for days without end, but You have also made all days in between now and then. *This day* is a day that You have given me. *Today* is a day to be glad and rejoice. I can't do that with eyes on what's going on and with a weighed-down mind. So I'll pray. Lift my eyes, Lord. Lift my mind. Lift my heart. Amen.

Rejoicing isn't a reflex. Rejoicing doesn't burst from us *only* when circumstances are just right. Rejoicing is a choice. God has made today, and we will rejoice in it!

LET ME SEE YOUR FACE

How long, O Lord? Will You forget me forever?
How long will You hide Your face from me?
PSALM 13:1 NLV

Lord, You hear my prayers. You've heard me as I've called out to You day after day with the same prayer. I'm seeking Your face, but I'm beginning to wonder if You've turned Your face from me. How long, Lord, will You hide Your face? How long will I look toward You only to feel that You are looking away? Still, I know You hear my every prayer, and I know You are with me. Do not hide Your face forever, Lord. I long to have the warmth of Your smile in my life again. I long to see You looking back at me. Amen.

It may seem that God has turned away from us, but His eyes are on us continually. "The eyes of the LORD are toward the righteous and his ears toward their cry" (Psalm 34:15 ESV). Keep crying, keep looking to Him.

OH GLORIOUS DAY!

*Yet what we suffer now is nothing compared
to the glory he will reveal to us later.*
ROMANS 8:18 NLT

So much is wrong, Lord. Everywhere, more and more, there is suffering. And my life—one among billions—has its share of suffering too. How do I break through this cloud of brokenness and pain and troubles to the clear sky beyond—where hope is? I need a new mindset. I need to lift my perspective from earth to heaven, from present problems to future glory. I need to raise my eyes to You. No amount of suffering, no matter how crushing, can compare to the glory that You will reveal, Lord. Fill my mind with a preview of the glory to come. Amen.

Weeping may last for the night, but joy comes with the morning (Psalm 30:5). Suffering may last through this life, but joy forevermore will come with eternity's dawning— with the bright Morning Star (Revelation 22:16).

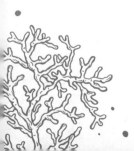

HOW'S YOUR EYESIGHT?

"Your eye is the lamp of your body. When your eye is healthy, your whole body is full of light, but when it is bad, your body is full of darkness. Therefore be careful lest the light in you be darkness."
LUKE 11:34–35 ESV

Jesus, You called our eyes lamps and said that healthy eyes let light into the body. But You weren't really talking about physical sight. I have a choice about what I "see," what I focus on with my heart too. And as I choose to look on Your truth, Your light shines into my center and spreads into every corner until my whole body becomes light filled! Until my whole life is lit—like a lamp's rays giving me light (Luke 11:36 ESV). Lord, keep my heart from looking on evil. Make my sight healthy, my spirit as a light. Amen.

The King James translation of Luke 11:34 is "the light of the body is the eye: therefore when thine eye is single, thy whole body also is full of light." You could say that a *singular* focus on God and His goodness brings light to our lives.

ANSWER THE CALL

Deep calls to deep in the roar of your waterfalls. . . .
By day the LORD directs his love, at night his song
is with me—a prayer to the God of my life.
PSALM 42:7–8 NIV

Lord, the closer I get to You, the more I realize how much I need You, how my soul depends on You like my lungs demand oxygen. So why do I drift from You? Why do I not stay close? It's never long before I feel the pull; it's never long before I sense the Spirit drawing me to You again. Like the deepest depths of the ocean calling at the sound of Your waterfalls, the deepest parts of me call out at the sound of Your voice. My soul responds to Your song, Lord. My inner being comes closer to be with You. Amen.

God promised, "I will put my Spirit in you and move you to follow [me]" (Ezekiel 36:27 NIV). As believers, Spirit calls to spirit. Are we calling back?

HAPPY ARE THEY

*Those who have a pure heart are
happy, because they will see God.*
MATTHEW 5:8 NLV

Lord, You began Your now famous Sermon on the Mount with a list of people who are blessed—happy. You said the pure in heart were happy because they would see God. Unlike unbelievers who cannot truly see You, I can see You through Your presence in my life. I can see You through Your Word. And one day in heaven, I will see You face to face. Lord, help me have a pure heart. Teach me to guard my heart and keep it unstained by the world. Show me what does not belong there. Because You're right—seeing You makes me happy! Amen.

Happy are the poor in spirit, the mourners, the meek, the persecuted. . . "The blessed" in Jesus' eyes aren't who we might expect, so we have to look through His eyes to see His blessing.

GLORY TO GLORY

We all, with unveiled face, beholding the glory of the Lord, are being transformed into the same image from one degree of glory to another. For this comes from the Lord who is the Spirit.

2 CORINTHIANS 3:18 ESV

God, since the day I became Your daughter, I have had access to You. I can come into Your presence, into a holy space, into a time of fellowship between the two of us. I can behold You with an unveiled face—nothing separates me from You, nothing keeps me from seeing Your glory. And as I behold Your glory, it slowly infuses me. I am changed degree by degree to be like the one I look upon. This is all from You, Lord. All thanks to You. All due to Your Spirit. All because You chose to look upon me. Amen.

We tend to reflect the ones we hang around—
our behavior matches theirs. Ditto with God:
when we spend time with God, we begin
to walk and talk and think just like Him.

AT HEART

"God testified concerning him: 'I have found David son of Jesse, a man after my own heart; he will do everything I want him to do.' "
ACTS 13:22 NIV

God, King David made mistakes, but he was still a man after Your own heart. His life was God-centered. I see it in his greatest moments and his worst. Like when David challenged Goliath, he did it because Goliath had defied You (1 Samuel 17:36). And when David sinned with Bathsheba, he said he had sinned against You and only You (Psalm 51:4). In my greatest moments, in my worst, and in all the other moments too, I want to live God-centered. Be the one I revolve around. Make my heart beat in time with Yours. Form me into a woman after Your own heart. Amen.

Often we unintentionally put God on the periphery because we get wrapped up in life. But what if we were more intentional about our prayer time? We'd likely get wrapped up in God!

FOR HIS NAME

Help us, God our Savior, for the glory of your name;
deliver us and forgive our sins for your name's sake.
PSALM 79:9 NIV

God, most times when I pray to You, it's personal. I'm asking for my own benefit. *Rescue me for me. Bless me for me. Forgive me for me. Help me for me.* I believe that You want to hear my unfiltered feelings, that You want me to pray without pretense. And I believe that You take pleasure in answering my prayers. But the things You do for me touch me then reach above me to where You are. Each answered prayer honors You. As You hear my prayers, Father, answer me for Your glory. Answer me for Your name's sake. Amen.

Jesus invites believers to pray in His name
(John 14:13–14), meaning not for ourselves but
for His purposes and praise. Many of us end our
prayers with "in Jesus' name. Amen." Why not
end with "for Jesus' name" as a reminder?

EVER AWAKE

Behold, he that keepeth Israel
shall neither slumber nor sleep.
PSALM 121:4 KJV

Lord, seemingly overnight or in the span of a single day, things change. For better and for worse. I find myself trying to think ahead, but that's pointless. For one thing, I can't see the future. For another thing, I don't have to! You, the one who keeps Israel, also keep me. You watch over me. And You neither slumber nor sleep. Your eyes are never closed to what is happening. Lord, You see it all *before* it happens, and You're using all of it to bring about Your will. I place myself in Your hands—He who keeps me, day and night. Amen.

Life events may seem like a bunch of colliding trains, but do not worry! God isn't asleep at the switch. Under His watchful eye, everything is on the right track and running on time.

KNOCK, KNOCK

*"I correct and discipline everyone I love.
So be diligent and turn from your indifference.
Look! I stand at the door and knock. If you hear
my voice and open the door, I will come in."*
REVELATION 3:19–20 NLT

God, the Laodiceans were lukewarm—not committed to You, not against You. And You wanted to get their attention. You told them that You stood at the door knocking—waiting for them to hear You and open the door to You. God, You won't allow the ones You love to do wrong without giving them a chance to do right. I am committed to You, but my life doesn't always line up with You. So You knock, knock, knock. Your Spirit rebukes, like invisible knuckles rapping on my spirit. Give me ears to hear You, God, and a heart to repent. Amen.

We could ignore God's call to repentance, but because
He knows that the pleasures of sin are not worth the
pain of disobedience, He will knock all the harder.

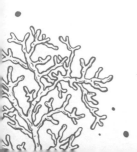

FROM ABOVE

*Whatever is good and perfect comes to us from
God. He is the One Who made all light. He does not
change. No shadow is made by His turning.*
JAMES 1:17 NLV

God, no matter how dark the day, the sun still shines. No matter how bad things get, there is still good. It may be hard to see, but if I look, I see it. When I see the good, I'm reminded of You—because, God, You are good! Not a speck of evil, no hint of bad is found in You. And in Your goodness, You send good things from Your heaven down to us. You are the origin of everything that is good and perfect. You are a steady point of goodness, of light. You are the greatest good even in the darkest day. Amen.

"Every good and perfect gift is from above" (James 1:17 NIV). The next time you spot one of God's gifts, be sure to look up and thank the giver.

THE SAVIOR'S PRAYERS

*He is able to save to the uttermost those who
draw near to God through him, since he always
lives to make intercession for them.*
HEBREWS 7:25 ESV

Jesus, You prayed for Your disciples individually, like the
time You prayed for Peter's faith not to fail (Luke 22:32). You
prayed for all Your followers as the hour of Your crucifixion
came (John 17:1–26). And You are still praying for us from
heaven. You are at the Father's side interceding on our behalf.
Through every test, through every temptation, through every
trial, I am never on my own. My prayers alone don't support
me—You are with me and for me, and You ever will be. Lord,
thank You for Your prayers. You know just how much they
mean to me. Amen.

Friends and family say they will pray for us,
but they may or may not. With Jesus, there is no
"may" about it: "Christ Jesus is the one. . .who is at
the right hand of God, who *indeed is* interceding
for us" (Romans 8:34 ESV, emphasis added).

CHILDLIKE

*"Let the little children come to me. . .for the
kingdom of God belongs to such as these. Truly I
tell you, anyone who will not receive the kingdom
of God like a little child will never enter it."*
LUKE 18:16–17 NIV

Who does the kingdom belong to? Lord, Your answer would probably surprise many people. Entering Your kingdom does not depend on a person being sophisticated or self-sufficient. You pointed to *little children* as our model—children who come to You in simplicity and helplessness; children who have nothing to offer You but themselves; children who are content just being near You. Lord, each year takes me further from childhood, but may I always be a child in Your presence. May I turn to You as a child looks to a parent. May I see Your open arms and run to be with You. Amen.

Childlike faith is a must. We're also told to grow up: "Like newborn babies, crave pure spiritual milk, so that by it you may grow up in your salvation" (1 Peter 2:2 NIV). Grow in your faith—but never lose your inner child.

HIGH HOPES

*Now faith is being sure we will get what we hope
for. It is being sure of what we cannot see.*
HEBREWS 11:1 NLV

Lord, my highest hope is the hope of heaven, a hope more solid than "I wish it will be." It is a sure hope—"I *know* it will be!" There are other hopes in my heart too. I hope in the promises of Your Word—the assurances that You are with me forever, that Your love is unbreakable, that You make good come from bad. But I also hope in the dreams You give me—the whispers of Your Spirit that my spirit alone can hear. Lord, weed out any false hope so that my only hopes are the ones You have planted in me. Amen.

Don't lose hope just because you cannot see your hopes taking shape: "Hope that is seen is no hope at all. . . . But if we hope for what we do not yet have, we wait for it patiently" (Romans 8:24–25 NIV).

CAPTIVE THOUGHTS

We. . .take every thought captive to obey Christ.
2 CORINTHIANS 10:5 ESV

God, You are Lord of lords and King of kings. You reign over the universe. You reign in my life—and You should rule my mind. But my thoughts can get away from me and run wild. A single thought is where the chaos starts, so Your Word says to take *every* thought captive—to grab hold of every thought that crosses my mind and make sure it falls in line with Your commands; to bring every wayward thought to You and ask Your help in changing my thoughts. God, create a desire in me to be obedient in what I do—and think. Amen.

Whether a thought of worry, hate, lust, jealousy, pride—you name it—a lone thought can become a host of thoughts that are hard to control. Take the first thought captive and turn it over to Jesus.

TO THE FULLEST

You must love the Lord your God with all your heart
and with all your soul and with all your strength.
DEUTERONOMY 6:5 NLV

God, Your greatest commandment sounds simple: Love You—
the one and only God—with all of me. With all my heart,
with all my soul, with all my strength. But a simple command
isn't always easy. I cringe to think that I have loved You
with just a part of my heart and soul and strength—and the
leftover part at that. Forgive me, God. You love me so fully,
and I don't want to love You back partially. Help me love as
You love, beginning right here in Your presence. I give You
my undivided attention, my undivided self, my undivided
love. Amen.

How do we love God? By keeping His commands,
commands that are not burdensome (1 John 5:3).
And—great news!—we are able to love God
because He is already loving us (1 John 4:19).

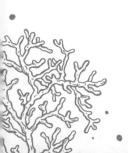

BETTER IS. . .

Better is one day in your courts than a thousand elsewhere; I would rather be a doorkeeper in the house of my God than dwell in the tents of the wicked.
PSALM 84:10 NIV

God, busy day follows busy day; and without me noticing it, the days become a long procession of places to go, people to see. But when I slow down and actually sit with You for a spell, I understand the psalmist's words. I realize that one day in Your presence beats thousands anywhere else. And, hands down, even just being at the edge of Your presence far surpasses being in the midst of the wicked. God, how blessed am I that You invite me to spend every day with You! How blessed am I that I will spend eternity with You! Amen.

Think of the best day of your life and multiply that by one thousand. Epic! But it still can't compare to one day with our God.

EARTHEN VESSEL, HEAVENLY TREASURE

*But we have this treasure in jars of clay to show that
this all-surpassing power is from God and not from us.*
2 CORINTHIANS 4:7 NIV

Lord, what a mess I am sometimes! Paul used an apt description when he called our human bodies jars of clay. I live in an imperfect, easily broken shell. But You chose me and many, many other jars of clay to hold a treasure. You placed Your light, Your truth, Your saving grace in us, so that the brilliance in us would shine on You. Lord, my jar of clay is feeling particularly rough and plain and weak today. Instead of keeping my mind on the jar, I will think on the treasure. I will look past myself and see You. Amen.

Clay jars were the disposables of biblical times.
Replaceable and cheap. Our bodies may be like
jars of clay, but to God we are irreplaceable and
far from cheap—we cost His Son's life.

WHENCE?

*I lift up my eyes to the hills. From where does
my help come? My help comes from the
Lord, who made heaven and earth.*
PSALM 121:1–2 ESV

Lord, centuries ago people probably looked to chariots for help. Today we still look to armies for protection, but we also look to money and technology to help us. Centuries ago the psalmist lifted his eyes to the hills and asked where his help came from. Today we lift our eyes to the sky and ask the same thing. And the answer is the same. Help comes from You. Lord, You know the help I need in this moment and in the moments ahead of me this week. Please lend Your hand as I lift my eyes to You, my help. Amen.

If our help comes from God, do we reject human
aid? Of course not. God uses humans to help
humans, but the one we bank on is Him.

IN HIM

"[God] is actually not far from each one of us,
for 'In him we live and move and have our being.' "
ACTS 17:27–28 ESV

God, sometimes I say I need to seek You; I say I need to draw near to You. But in reality You are close to me. I don't have to travel far to find You. I don't have to move at all to be next to You. For You are the very life within me. In You I live, I move, I am. In You are breath and energy and existence. I can't comprehend all Your nuances—all that You are. You are too marvelous for me to wrap my brain around, but I know well enough to open my heart to You. Amen.

There is not a place where God is not.
The great I Am is where we are. We have
only to look up to share our hearts with Him.

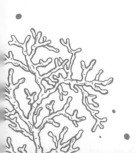

THE HEART FIRST

"Do not consider his appearance or his height, for I have rejected him. The LORD does not look at the things people look at. People look at the outward appearance, but the LORD looks at the heart."
1 SAMUEL 16:7 NIV

Lord, when I look in the mirror, what I see are flaws, and then I think negatively about myself because I'm not as beautiful as other women. But when You look at me, You don't zero in on the flaws; You see straight to my heart. Lord, You've always esteemed the heart. You sent Samuel to anoint the next king, and Samuel thought Eliab must be the one, probably because he was handsome and tall. You, however, chose a king who had a king's heart. Lord, help me form new opinions of myself based on who I am *inside*. Amen.

People look at the outside and work their way in—from what a person looks like to what a person *is* like. But God turns that order inside out. He starts with the heart.

WHAT'S YOUR DESIRE?

Take delight in the LORD, and he will
give you the desires of your heart.
PSALM 37:4 NIV

Lord, today my heart seems full of unfulfilled desires. Your Word reminds me that You are able to meet those desires, but I'm almost as full of doubt as I am of desire. Can I really trust You to give me the desires of my heart? What if my desires aren't Your will for me, aren't what You desire in my life? But Your Word reminds me of something else too—that You are my first desire. As I delight myself in Your presence, the desires that I still have will be fulfilled by the one who knows my heart's desires better than I know them myself. Amen.

If we don't find happiness in the Lord, it won't make any difference how many other desires are satisfied—we will be unsatisfied. Our greatest desire will remain.

MAKE MUSIC

*It is good to give thanks to the Lord, and sing praises
to Your name, O Most High. It is good to tell of Your
loving-kindness in the morning, and of how faithful You
are at night, with harps, and with music of praise.*
PSALM 92:1–3 NLV

God, it is good to worship You with music, to sing praises
to You. My soul feels how good it is each week when Your
church gathers together. Cares don't hold me down when
my voice is raised in song. Life doesn't seem as complicated
with a melody of Your truth in my heart. Yes, God, it is good
to worship You with music, to sing praises to You; and it is
good *every* day. Morning or night, humming, strumming, or
belting out the notes, I will use music to lift my soul and exalt
Your name, O Most High! Amen.

Not a singer? Can't play an instrument? No worries!
Listening to worshipful music is an excellent option
that honors God and keeps our spirits looking up.

HOW TO FLOURISH

The righteous will flourish like a palm tree, they will grow like a cedar of Lebanon; planted in the house of the LORD, they will flourish in the courts of our God.
PSALM 92:12–13 NIV

To flourish like a palm. To grow like a cedar. God, I want those things to be true of my life. I want to thrive. But thriving only happens in one condition, and it has nothing to do with my life situation—whether my days are sunny or gray, whether I'm in plenty or poverty, whether I'm sick or well. I can thrive in the middle of a storm, in a season of drought, or even after being uprooted, as long as I am in Your presence, as long as I am near my God. And near You I can always be. Amen.

A tree planted in the right soil grows, but without the soil it withers. It's the same concept when our lives are planted in God's soil—His Word, His presence. With God we flourish; apart from Him we don't.

HOSPITABLE

*Be not forgetful to entertain strangers: for thereby
some have entertained angels unawares.*
HEBREWS 13:2 KJV

Lord, entertaining can be stressful, especially when I don't know my guests very well. I'm tempted to ignore this call to hospitality. I can think of many excuses *not* to invite others over. Lord, don't let me be forgetful, because hospitality is important to You. Whether my hospitality is a simple dinner or a bigger sacrifice of time and space, it isn't just about a meal or a place to stay. I'm welcoming people as You welcomed me. I'm opening the door for You to work in astounding ways. Help my heart to be hospitable, Lord, so my home will be too. Amen.

Entertaining strangers isn't necessarily a solo venture. If you're married, obviously you'll want to plan with your spouse! If you're single, get creative with your friends or roommates. Ask God to show you ways to show hospitality.

OH LOVE!

"Greater love has no one than this: to lay down one's life for one's friends. You are my friends if you do what I command."
JOHN 15:13–14 NIV

Lord, maybe it's because of the movies we watch or the books we read. Maybe it's just inborn. But women—myself included—often idealize love and romance. We dream of happily ever after. Sometimes I even idolize love and romance. Without it, life is empty—or at least blah. Yet there is no greater love than sacrificial love, and even if I had no human love in my life, You have shown me the greatest love. You love me completely, unconditionally, perfectly. I need to look up for love first, Lord. Then with a heart fully loved, I can give—and receive—love fully. Amen.

It doesn't matter how our love story reads— whether we're single, married, widowed, divorced—love must come from above before love will ever be enough down here on earth.

GIVING HONOR

Honor the Lord with your riches, and with the first of all you grow. Then your store-houses will be filled with many good things.
PROVERBS 3:9–10 NLV

Lord, my bank balance is close to hitting rock bottom. You know it, I know. You also know how tempting it is for me to neglect my offerings when I have little to give from. I want to hold on to every penny. But Lord, even now I am wealthy compared to a lot of people. Though not much, I have money to give, and no gift is too minuscule for You to multiply it. May I honor You, Lord, with my firstfruits. May my faithful giving show that I don't trust in riches—I trust in my God, who richly provides. Amen.

Jesus praised a widow who put two coins into the temple treasury (Mark 12:41–44). The amount of our offering isn't important. The amount of our faith is.

WISDOM FROM GOD

The wisdom that comes from heaven is first of all pure.
Then it gives peace. It is gentle and willing to obey.
It is full of loving-kindness and of doing good. It has no
doubts and does not pretend to be something it is not.
JAMES 3:17 NLV

God, I think there's a saying that says life wouldn't be so hard if it wasn't for other people. It's challenging to get along with others as I get along in life. Jealousy and ambition lead to tension. Fights stir up trouble. We need wisdom for living in harmony with each other. And not just any wisdom—godly wisdom, the wisdom that comes from You. God, teach me how to interact with people using wisdom that is pure, peaceable, considerate, merciful, sincere. Give me courage to live with that kind of wisdom whether the people around me are or not. Amen.

In a sticky situation with another person?
Before venting to a friend, before asking a
sister's advice, seek God's counsel. Talk with
Him. Look for the wisdom from heaven.

185

REVIVED!

For this is what the high and exalted One says. . . "I live in a high and holy place, but also with the one who is contrite and lowly in spirit, to revive the spirit of the lowly and to revive the heart of the contrite."
ISAIAH 57:15 NIV

Lord, You are high above me. I'm never more aware of that than when I'm feeling low—not down-in-the-dumps low, but scum-of-the-earth low. You are holier than me, and I could never reach Your heights alone. But although You are lofty, You live with the lowly. You are with me even as I call to You from this low place. You are near and willing to revive me! Lord, renew my heart; refresh my spirit. Lift the weight of my sins from me so that I can once again lift my face to You, the high and exalted one. Amen.

Our spirits can be depleted any day of the week, not just on our sinful days. God's presence is the refreshment we need. He's the breath that gives a second (and third and fourth. . .) wind to our souls.

186

IS ANYONE SICK?

*Is any sick among you? let him call for the elders
of the church; and let them pray over him. . . .
And the prayer of faith shall save the sick,
and the Lord shall raise him up.*
JAMES 5:14–15 KJV

Lord, someone I care about is sick. I feel helpless. How do I combat something that is invisible yet causes so much pain? I see it etched on my friend's face—the fear, the hurting. But Lord, we are never helpless, even when medicine fails. We are not hopeless, even when the diagnosis is bleak. We are not beat, because we have not begun until we come together *and pray*. Lord, You have power over every disease and power over death. Hear this prayer. Hear our prayers of faith in the coming days. Hear and heal. Raise this friend up. Amen.

The power of prayer isn't in the prayer itself—
in the words we speak. The power is in the
hearer Himself—in the one we pray to. Have
faith in God's power and God's providence.

HONEST?

*God can't stomach liars; he loves the
company of those who keep their word.*
PROVERBS 12:22 MSG

God, honesty is no small thing to You. After all, You sent Truth
to earth so that we could be set free by knowing the truth
(John 8:32). I'm going to be honest with You right now, God.
Honesty can be an issue with me. Maybe I don't lie outright.
But I'll say yes to doing things despite a niggling that I won't
be able to do them. And my posts on social media can be
less than truthful, just so I'll look good. If I can't be honest,
let me be silent! Because, God, You hate lying (Proverbs
6:16–17), but You love being with the upright. Amen.

Honesty with others requires tact. It requires
practice if lying is a habit. And honesty requires
honesty. Take a hard look at your life, and ditch
dishonesty with the help of God's truth.

PRAYERFUL WHEN FEARFUL

*I looked for the Lord, and He answered
me. And He took away all my fears.*
PSALM 34:4 NLV

Lord, as a little girl, I was afraid of thunderstorms and dark
basements and spiders. Now that I'm older, my fears aren't
the same. But—while I don't hide under the covers or behind
a couch when a storm rolls through, while I can walk into a
basement without any lights on, and while I only freak out
over *big* spiders—I still become afraid. And the fear is as
potent as ever. I'm a little girl again inside. So Lord, I call to
You when I'm afraid. I cry, "Abba!" and You answer. I bring
You my fears in prayer, and You take away the fear. Amen.

Fears come in many shapes and sizes.
But whatever the cause of our fear, God is our
comfort. Whether they're real or imagined,
rational or irrational, God removes *all* fears.

TO OLD AGE AND BEYOND

"Even to your old age I am he, and to gray hairs I will carry you. I have made, and I will bear; I will carry and will save."
ISAIAH 46:4 ESV

Lord, sometimes I wonder what my life will be like if You grant me long years. I worry too about what will happen as I get older. Will I have health issues? Will I be left alone? Lord, I leave all my concerns with You. You have been caring for me since before I was born. You have been walking with me every day since then. And You do not change even as age changes me. You will bear me until my last breath and carry me into heaven. So I will rest in the arms that hold my life. I will trust in You. Amen.

Aging may be a burden, but as with all burdens, we are not meant to shoulder it alone: "Cast your burden on the LORD, and he will sustain you" (Psalm 55:22 ESV).

IN PROPORTION

My Christian brothers, you know everyone should listen much and speak little. He should be slow to become angry. A man's anger does not allow him to be right with God.
JAMES 1:19–20 NLV

Listen much. Speak little. Be slow to become angry. Lord, that's good advice—and pretty much opposite of our culture. We talk a lot and listen very little. We are quick to vent, quick to form grudges, quick to get angry. And that's quite the opposite of You, Lord. You are slow to anger, abounding in love (Psalm 86:15). You listen to us much more than we listen to You. I don't want our relationship to be out of joint because of anger. Help me follow Your ways and Your Word. Help me listen more, speak less, and be quick to love. Amen.

Tempers flaring isn't a modern malady. The book of Proverbs is sprinkled with verses about anger, including this one: "Good sense makes one slow to anger, and it is his glory to overlook an offense" (Proverbs 19:11 ESV).

DECISIONS, DECISIONS

The Leveler evens the road for the right-living.
We're in no hurry, GOD. We're content to linger
in the path sign-posted with your decisions.
ISAIAH 26:7–8 MSG

God, this decision that lies before me—I just don't know what to decide! I have a couple of choices, and the one I choose makes a difference. Whether I go left or right, my life will change. This isn't the time to rush. It's a time to be still, a time to quiet my thoughts so that You can get through to me. Give me patience to wait for Your go-ahead. Let me see clearly the direction You have marked out. Settle my mind on the decision that is Your will. God, set my feet on the path You have leveled before me. Amen.

We're good at overcomplicating decision making, when God's method is uncomplicated. Prayerfully ask for His guidance, and then *trust*. Trust Him to make the path straight. Trust Him to close doors and open them. Trust Him to lead you by His Spirit.

DISCONNECTED

Just thinking of my troubles and my lonely wandering
makes me miserable. . . . Then I remember something
that fills me with hope. The LORD's kindness never fails!
LAMENTATIONS 3:19, 21–22 CEV

Lord, I read the words *lonely wandering* and picture the author, likely Jeremiah, trekking across the desert. I picture a journey through a windswept, desolate land without a friendly face in sight. My life doesn't look like that, but it can *feel* like that. Loneliness can show up in crowded spaces. Friends are a click away, yet we're walking through life far apart. Lord, in the middle of his misery Jeremiah remembered. Misery became hope in light of Your kindness. Your kindness, Lord, is unfailing toward me too. Look on my troubles and bring into my life the flesh-and-blood friendships I need. Amen.

God forms us through our friendships and through our loneliness. Lonely days—and lonely seasons— are not errors in God's design or oversights in His planning. Watch for God's hand wherever you are.

NO ROOM FOR DOUBT

*My friends, watch out! Don't let evil thoughts or
doubts make any of you turn from the living God.*
HEBREWS 3:12 CEV

God, to the world, Your Word is nonsense; to unbelievers,
belief in You is folly. John the Baptist said humans can receive
nothing "except it be given. . .from heaven" (John 3:27 KJV).
Truly, without Your insight, some of the things I read in the
Bible would seem too fantastic to be believed. I have faith,
God, but during trials or temptations, my faith is vulner-
able. A word, a thought—a hint of doubt—could make me
question You, then turn from You. Don't let me let that happen!
Fill my mind so full of Your truth that any doubt just won't
fit. Amen.

Doubt was Eve's first downfall. The serpent asked,
"Did God really say. . . ?" and the rest is history. The
devil still whispers doubts in our ears. The question
is whether we will listen to him or to God.

MERRY HEARTS

*A merry heart doeth good like a medicine:
but a broken spirit drieth the bones.*
PROVERBS 17:22 KJV

God, I wonder if the expression "Laughter is the best medicine" has roots in the Bible. Proverbs says that a merry heart works like medicine—it does a body good! It's the joke told by a friend that lightens the mood and dries the tears. It's the glad spirit that looks on the bright side of a dark day. It's the fun memories that gradually blot out the heartache. It's the cheerfulness that carries us through gloom. God, thank You for laughter. Thank You for hearts made to be merry. I'll take a dose of that medicine today! Amen.

Laughter is good medicine. Laughter is also
contagious and not something you have to
be afraid to spread around. Go ahead—share
a chuckle or maybe even a belly laugh.

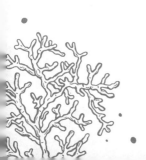

WORKABLE

Farmers who wait for perfect weather never plant.
If they watch every cloud, they never harvest.
ECCLESIASTES 11:4 NLT

Lord, the mound of tasks I have to do is growing. Some of the projects are so massive I don't know where to dive in. So rather than tackling any of the work, I put it off. I busy myself with things that don't need to be done to avoid doing the things that do need to be done. Then by day's end I'm more overwhelmed than ever. Lord, I need to divide the work and conquer it. I need to break it into manageable chunks. I need to stop contemplating the work and start working. Please guide me with Your wisdom as I get to work! Amen.

Breaking down big jobs is a tactic as old as creation.
Really. The biggest job ever was creation, and
God did the work in six days, stage by stage.

JUST PERFECT

Nothing is completely perfect, except your teachings.
I deeply love your Law! I think about it all day.
PSALM 119:96–97 CEV

Lord, before an event or a vacation or anything else happening, I build up in my mind what I expect it to be like. Often those expectations are high. I want things to go smoothly—perfectly. It's the same with most things I do, actually. I aim for perfection. But as often as I have high expectations, I experience disappointment. Does anything live up to the buildup? Lord, only Your words are perfect. Only You live up to—and exceed—my highest expectation. With my mind built up in *You*, the rest of life, well, it doesn't have to be perfect. Amen.

Frame your day with prayer—and take God's
words with you through the hours in between—
and you'll be amazed by how even the splotches
in life blend to create something beautiful.

PROBE YOUR HEART

*Stand in awe, and sin not: commune with your
own heart upon your bed, and be still.*
Psalm 4:4 kjv

Darkness drapes my room and silence softens the night. Lord, Your Word says to commune with my own heart and be still. Thoughts are churning in my mind, but that isn't the same as communing with my heart. My body lies here, muscles static, but that isn't the same as being still. Lord, quiet my inner restlessness. Teach me to meditate in my heart. I'm skilled at glossing over but not at going deep. Shine Your light into darkness. Speak to me in the silence. Make known to me my heart of hearts and conform it to Yours. I stand in awe of You, Lord. Amen.

Meditation, reflection, pondering—they all call
for concentration, an ability that our sound-bite
multimedia world doesn't foster. But prayer
does. God's presence settles us, stills us,
until we're fully focused on Him.

EXALTED AMONG THE NATIONS

*"Step out of the traffic! Take a long, loving look at me,
your High God, above politics, above everything."*
PSALM 46:10 MSG

God, politics are dividing our nation. Political issues can even drive a wedge between friends, between family, between siblings in Christ. Participating in elections, being aware of current issues, taking a stand for what is right—that's important, but it's not most important. I pledge allegiance to my country, but I pledge my life to You, my God, who is above all nations, above the whole earth, above any political party. God, You command me to love *people*, not politics. Help me "step out of the traffic," out of the middle of the conflict, so that I can be love on either side of the divide. Amen.

Two sides of an issue and two opposing
candidates often represent right and wrong to us.
We're passionate about the right and as passionately
against the wrong. But we need to control our passion,
trusting that, win or lose, God is in control too.

EARTH ON LOAN

The Scriptures say, "The earth and everything in it belong to the Lord."
1 CORINTHIANS 10:26 CEV

Lord God, when You created our earth, You created a place of beauty and wonder. I could spend many minutes thanking You for the beauty and wonder in Your creation. Like sunset ombré skies; hushed cathedral-like forests; canyons and mountains that are so unbelievably big, they seem painted across the landscape; ocean waves, at once powerful and soothing. All of it is Yours, Lord. All of it You graciously share with me. Sometimes we, Your human creation, literally trash Your world. Lord, lead me in preserving it. What can I do to take care of the beauty and wonder You created? Amen.

Conserve water. Pick up litter. Recycle. Volunteer at a nature center. Plant trees. Drive less. Those earth-loving ideas may seem inconsequential, but even simple things have a ripple effect.

THE AVENGER

Dear friends, never avenge yourselves.
Leave that to God, for he has said that
he will repay those who deserve it.
ROMANS 12:19 TLB

God, I'm so mad I could scream! This person hurt me, yet she's getting off the hook. God, You saw what happened. You saw everything leading up to it, and You see everything that follows. You see everything that I cannot see. You see motives that are underneath the surface; You see what this one incident is bringing about. And Your revenge will be justice, God, because You act fairly. I'll only act selfishly. So I leave it to You. I step back and let You move in Your way and Your time. Avenge me, God, as You see fit. Amen.

A person inflicts harm on us—or worse— on someone we love. We take it personally, so we might also think, *Vengeance is mine.* But vengeance is *His.* Don't dish out even a penny's worth of revenge. God will repay.

A PRAYER FOR (IN)SIGHT

*Open my eyes that I may see
wonderful things in your law.*
PSALM 119:18 NIV

Lord, before I open Your Word, I need to ask You to open my eyes. I don't do this often enough; I usually plunge right into my reading. But Lord, You breathed out every word, and if not for Your Spirit whispering to me, the words would just be words. So in the quiet moments while my Bible is still closed, I will ask You to make my heart ready to receive Your truth. Make my mind ready to understand. Make my spirit ready to obey. And then, Lord, open my eyes to see the wonderful things in scripture, all that You want to say to me in Your Word. Amen.

The author, who knows every letter and punctuation mark of scripture, is waiting to help us through every last word. *Open our eyes, Lord! Open our eyes to see.*

"SEEK MY FACE"

You have said, "Seek my face." My heart says
to you, "Your face, Lord, do I seek."
PSALM 27:8 ESV

Lord, it is an amazing thing that You call to me. I wouldn't look for You on my own; I would continue being lost. I wouldn't come to You in prayer; I wouldn't know You were there listening! But You *have* called to me. You have said, "Seek My face," and my heart says back, "Your face do I seek." Oh, sometimes I feel You calling to me—during a hectic day or when I've gone too long without a good long talk with You— and I ignore the tug. Please call to me yet: *"Seek My face."* Keep calling until my heart, Lord, seeks Your face. Amen.

How much pain will be eased, how many burdens
lifted, how many temptations overcome, how much
confusion cleared, how many blessings bestowed
if we hear God say, "Pray," and we pray?

SHORT AND SINCERE

*Do not be quick with your mouth, do not be hasty in
your heart to utter anything before God. God is in heaven
and you are on earth, so let your words be few.*
ECCLESIASTES 5:2 NIV

God, with each prayer, help me weigh my words. I am talking to
You—God in heaven—from earth below. You—the Almighty—
hear these words I'm saying in my heart. And I don't have to
pile on words for You to hear me either, because You know
my prayers, my needs, before one word is spoken (Matthew
6:7–8). You know the words that are earnest and the words
that are empty. You understand me without any words at all!
So here I am before You, God, meaning what I pray, letting
my words be few. Amen.

You're not alone if "prayer time" means kneeling
to pray then getting up and going as soon as
"Amen" crosses your lips. But imagine: Prayer can
be more than our words. Prayer can be a time of
one-on-one, soul-deep conversation with God.

LOOK UP!

They asked each other, "Who will roll the stone away from the entrance of the tomb?" But when they looked up, they saw that the stone, which was very large, had been rolled away.
MARK 16:3–4 NIV

God, the first day of the week arrived, the sun was still weak in the sky, and three women made their way to the tomb. Likely their hearts were downcast and so were their eyes as they walked along. They'd hardly reached the tomb, and already they predicted an obstacle—that unwieldy, unyielding stone! *But when they looked up*, they saw that You had done what they couldn't. God, my heart is downcast, my eyes too, envisioning the obstacles ahead of me. *"Look up!"* You're saying, *"See Me—the one who rolls away obstacles."* And so I look up. Amen.

Death was no match for God; neither are any of the stones in our path, be they boulders or pebbles. Remember, faith can move entire mountains (Matthew 17:20).

BEGINNING AND END

"I am the Alpha and the Omega, the first and the last, the beginning and the end."
REVELATION 22:13 ESV

Lord God, You have told me that You are the Alpha and the Omega. You are the First and the Last. You are the Beginning and the End. You are a God—*the* God—who was, who is, and who will forever be. Wherever I am in my life history, Your presence stands like towers in a suspension bridge. You hem me in behind and before, with Your guiding, guarding hand on me (Psalm 139:5). Never will there be a moment when I cannot look up to find You with me. And never will there be a prayer that You do not hear. Amen.

God is past and future, and God is present. He is here now. God wants us to draw close. He waits for us to share what is on our hearts. So why are *you* waiting? Look up!

MORE INSPIRATION FOR YOUR LOVELY HEART

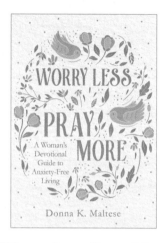

Worry Less, Pray More

This purposeful devotional guide features 180 readings and prayers designed to help alleviate your worries as you learn to live in the peace of the Almighty God, who offers calm for your anxiety-filled soul. *Worry Less, Pray More* reinforces the truth that, with God, you can live anxiety-free every single day—whether you worry about your work, relationships, bills, the turmoil of the world, or something more.

Paperback / 978-1-68322-861-5